Rakhmaninov

Rakhmaninov

Andreas Wehrmeyer

translated by Anne Wyburd
preface by Aaron Shorr

HAUS PUBLISHING · LONDON

First published in German in the Rowohlt monographien
series © 2000 Rowohlt Taschenbuch Verlag GmbH

This English translation first published in Great Britain
in 2004 by Haus Publishing Limited
26 Cadogan Court
Draycott Avenue
London
SW3 3BX

English translation© Anne Wyburd, 2004

The moral right of the author has been asserted

A CIP catalogue record for this book is available from the British Library

ISBN 1-904341-50-0 (paperback)

Typeset by Lobster Design
Printed and bound by Graphicom in Vicenza, Italy

Cover image: The Lebrecht Music Collection
Back cover: The Lebrecht Music Collection
Page iii: The Lebrecht Music Collection

Contents

Preface

'Do you believe that a composer can have real genius, sincerity, profundity of feeling, and at the same time be popular?'

This remarkable question, posed to Rakhmaninov by the *Boston Globe* critic, Olin Downes, encapsulates some of the enormous hostility that Rakhmaninov suffered at the hands of his contemporary critics. In fact, Rakhmaninov's own powers of self-criticism were formidable, and the assistance of musical inferiors to sow further self-doubt on his compositional worth was unnecessary. Frequent bouts of depression and periods of artistic silence attest to the inner struggles of his art. While all musicians are laid bare to the subjective critiques of their contemporaries, the attacks on Rakhmaninov were particularly vehement, ultimately defining the battle lines for the advancement of new music. Critical opinion was largely massed against the music of Rakhmaninov; thus, seeing off the 'last of the Romantics'. World war, revolution, pandemic and depression created the emotional backdrop to the rhythm and harmony of the new modernist musical language. Dissonance, atonality, anguish and conflict were now artistically relevant; the critics awaited the response of so great a musician as Rakhmaninov – eventually becoming impatient with his seeming musical intransigence and reactionary artistic response to the prevailing world mood. It has

> Great music is written from the depths of the soul. The great artist attempts to recreate beauty by transforming his feelings into music. Music is weakened by concerns about how others may feel about it. 'In art the struggle is more often against oneself alone and victories so achieved are perhaps the finest.'
> Debussy

often been commented that Rakhmaninov's misfortune was living so long into the 20th century, irking the modernists with every passing year with the survival of his titanic profile as the pre-eminent concert artist of his day.

Rakhmaninov once paraphrased an old Russian proverb, *I tried to chase three hares, but did I catch any of them?* The 'three hares' were, of course, his careers as pianist, conductor and composer. In the first two, Rakhmaninov was unsurpassed. He was fêted by the greatest musicians of the day and there was no engagement he could not command throughout the world.

His career as a conductor was mostly known in Russia, where he eventually became the director of the Bolshoi Theatre. He was renowned for his mastery of detail and inflexible disciplinary regime, cleaning up aeons of musical malpractice and indifference. Medtner went so far as to declare him the greatest of all conductors, surpassing even Nikisch in his interpretation of Tchaikovsky's symphonies. Rakhmaninov the conductor stripped his interpretations of all mannerisms and preconceptions, and this differed somewhat from his interpretative approach on the piano, which generally allowed for a more spontaneous treatment of rhythm.

In his career as a concert pianist, Rakhmaninov's impact was unparalleled. He was rightly hailed as the greatest pianist of his day and served as the benchmark of 20th-century piano playing. The honour roll of great artists testifying to his pianistic genius unquestionably sealed his legendary status. For Horovitz, he was a piano god. Schnabel, the first to record all the Beethoven Sonatas, surprisingly declared that Rakhmaninov was the greatest of all Beethoven interpreters. Josef Hofmann wrote, 'Rakhmaninov was made of steel and gold; steel in his arms, gold in his heart. I can never think of this majestic being without tears in my eyes, for I not only admired him as a supreme artist, but I also loved him as a man. The world had never known a purer or more saintly soul than Rakhmaninov and this was the only reason why he had become a great musician, whereas the fact that he had such magnificent fingers was purely incidental.' Even Stravinsky, who disliked his music, declared that as a pianist he was awesome.

Rakhmaninov's overwhelming artistic presence and mesmeric pianism propelled his compositions onto the world stage. However, the debates swirling around his compositions are copious and historically significant, representing Modernism's search for spiritual, formal and harmonic justification – all at the inevitable expense of the waning 19th-century tradition. A cursory glance at the diversity of composers working during Rakhmaninov's lifetime reveal epic, 'Darwinian' forces at work as a new epoch of music emerged: Tchaikovsky, Rimsky-Korsakov, Scriabin, Brahms, Reger, Debussy, Ravel, Stravinsky, Schoenberg, Webern, Prokofiev, Bartók, Shostakovich, Hindemith, Strauss, Puccini, Gershwin! In this light, it is all the more remarkable that Rakhmaninov's music found any oxygen for existence! The fact that it has found permanency in the musical canon is a testament to its more profound intrinsic values, transcending comparisons with similar music of lesser stature – usually found in the virtuoso concerto vehicles and encore 'fluff' so commonplace to the armoury of touring virtuosi of that age. No amount of criticism, geographical divide, cultural diversity or musical prejudice could impede its worldwide proliferation. This public success was a particular sore point with many critics. V. Karatygin wrote: 'Rakhmaninov's music corresponds, as it were, to the arithmetically average criterion of taste of the broad public. It pays homage to him because in his music Rakhmaninov has somehow managed to hit the bull's-eye of philistine musical taste. Rakhmaninov's talent always moves along a tangent to art, only lightly touching its sphere and never penetrating into it. An impressive splendour of external finish combined with worthless content is a typical feature of most of Rakhmaninov's works. They are terribly sincere. Everywhere one senses the vital experience of certain, for the most part, highly pathetic, emotions. But they are crude and shallow and affected these experiences.'

His was music of the past, but uncannily well adapted to an uncertain future. How Rakhmaninov conjured this artistic universality in defiance of musical fashion is one of the great allures of his music. Rakhmaninov's oeuvre has proven to be inextinguishable and utterly fascinating, partly because of its contradictions and fallibilities but ultimately for its ingenious melodic imagination, opulent harmonic palette, gripping dramatic force and discernible originality.

In deciphering the enigmatic fabric of Rakhmaninov's music, several recurrent themes warrant consideration. Crucially, Rakhmaninov's music was to become a sounding board for Russia, its people, animated language, panoramic landscape – its struggles, aspirations and enormous passions. His music was Russian to the core but without lapsing into overt folk references. Ernest Newman commented, 'Superficially he is perhaps less national than the composers who coquet with Russian folk music. But in a deeper sense he is perhaps more national than they. His sombreness is the purest vintage of a wine that is to be found only in the more pessimistic of the Russian poets. He is more truly in the line of the pure Russian culture succession than Borodin or Rimsky-Korsakov, who often wrote as if Russian literature hardly existed.'

Additionally, the Russian soul alluded to by Newman was bared most clearly in his outpouring of lyricism. The ability to sing simply, nobly, without inhibition, in long soaring lines, graced all of his music. He attached great importance to the composition of melody. In particular, for pianists of the 20th century, abundance of melody, and its consequent yearning for adequate harmonization became a diminishing resource as percussive and fragmented utterances gained prominence in modernist circles. Successful, *idiomatic* treatment of the piano is a skill that eludes many great composers and cannot be underestimated in any overall assessment. Just running one's hands through a Rakhmaninov creation is to feel pianistic genius at work. All pianists, whether amateur or professional, are privileged to feel the Rakhmaninov hand, its stretch, power, ingenuity, lyricism, mechanism and structure, in every passage – it is inescapable and incessantly fascinating. Interestingly, Rakhmaninov had similar sentiments concerning Chopin's art, revelling in its tactile beauty. *Chopin! From the time when I was nineteen years old, I felt his greatness and I marvel at it still. He is today more modern than many moderns. It is incredible that he should remain so modern. His genius is so tremendous that not any composer of today is more modern in style, and he remains for me one of the greatest of the giants...Would that another Chopin might arise to bring new pianistic beauties to the world! Notwithstanding all the playing I do during the course of the year, I find myself continually playing Chopin at home, just for the sheer pleasure of the thing. There is a delight in letting one's fingers run through his perfectly moulded passages. Every note seems to be just where it belongs to produce the finest effect, and not one seems to be out of place. There is nothing to add and nothing to take away.*

Rakhmaninov was deeply distressed by the loss of his homeland. His self-imposed exile following the tumult of the 1917 Revolution exacted a high price on his compositional output. He produced only six major works, plus a handful of transcriptions, during the last twenty-five years of his life – a remarkable fact considering how crucial composing was to his very existence. Except for his 'Paganini Rhapsody', which did enjoy popular and critical success, the 3rd Symphony, Symphonic Dances, Corelli Variations and revised 4th Piano Concerto were all greeted with what was by now customary critical derision. In the face of such musical opposition, Rakhmaninov famously kept his feelings private, shying away from all discussions and interviews on contemporary trends in music, for fear of causing further insult to powerful enemies. His compositions were his manifesto on art. They needed no further prose, preface or apology. He did, however, venture one exception to this rule when he replied to *The Musical Courier* on a question about contemporary music.

"I feel like a ghost wandering in a world grown alien. I cannot cast out the old way of writing, and I cannot acquire the new. I have made intense effort to feel the musical manner of today, but it will not come to me. Unlike Madame Butterfly with her quick religious conversion, I cannot cast out my musical gods in a moment and bend the knee to new ones. Even with the disaster of living through what has befallen the Russia where I spent my happiest years, yet I always feel that my own music and my reactions to all music, remained spiritually the same, unendingly obedient in trying to create beauty…

The new kind of music seems to come, not from the heart, but from the head. Its composers think rather than feel. They have not the capacity to make their works 'exult,' as Hans von Bülow called it. They mediate, protest, analyse, reason, calculate, and brood – but they do not exult. It may be that they compose in the spirit of the times; but it may be, too, that the spirit of the times does not call for expression in music. If that is the case, rather than compile music that is thought but not felt, composers should remain silent and leave contemporary expression to those authors and playwrights who are masters of the factual and literal, and do not concern themselves with the state of the soul.

I hope that with these thoughts I have answered your question regarding my opinion of what is called modern music. Why modern in this case? It grows old almost as soon as born, for it comes into being contaminated with dry rot.

Is it necessary to add that I do not mind telling you all this confidentially as a friend, but that I should not in any circumstances like you to publish it – at least, not while I am alive, for I should not enjoy having some of the 'modernists' rap me over the fingers, as I need them for my piano playing. It is not politic for me even to have written to you as I have.

I mostly keep my opinions to myself, and in consequence I am generally regarded as a silent man. So be it. In silence lies safety.

Rakhmaninov not only represented one of Romanticism's last great advocates, but he also stood at the end of a long tradition of truly great performing composers. The last decades of the 19th century saw the paths of composers and performers splintering into highly professional but increasingly compartmentalised disciplines. Rakhmaninov's traumatic break with his early piano mentor, Zverev, in order to concentrate more seriously on composition, challenged the emerging 'hothouse' method of musical training at the expense of music creation and; thus, deeper interpretative insight. The composer/performer divide became further entrenched in the 20th century, resulting in performers who are unaware of compositional craft and composers who are unfamiliar with the struggles of instrumental mastery at the highest level and, most importantly, the art of public performance. Audience popularity and compositional integrity might even be considered conflicts of interest, as was suggested by Olin Downes.

Rakhmaninov commented, *If you are a composer you have an affinity with other composers. You can make contact with their imaginations, knowing something of their problems and ideals. You can give their works colour. That is the most important thing for me in my pianoforte interpretations, colour. So you can make music live. Without colour it is dead…The great interpreters in the past were composers in most instances. Paganini, so we understand, and in our time Paderewski and Kreisler. Ah! I know what you are thinking. But it doesn't matter. It makes no difference whether these are first- or fourth-rate composers. What matters is they had the creative mind and so were able to communicate with other minds of the same order.*

Rakhmaninov's musical cul-de-sac still provides an unending resource to musicians of the new millennium. It just could not fade and die away, as was so audaciously predicted in Eric Blom's now notorious article on Rakhmaninov for the 5th edition of

Grove's Dictionary in 1954. Its soul and inspired lyricism are unquenchable. While the late Romantic creations of his contemporaries, Scriabin, Medtner, Ziloti and Godowsky, have all undergone various stages of vital resurrection and rediscovery, Rakhmaninov never left the world stage for a moment. The enormous artistic and technical demands presented in his works continue to appeal to subsequent generations of musicians. The musicologist Deryck Cooke commented that, 'because of continued enthusiasm by both performers and listeners ... Rakhmaninov remains within our musical experience despite the most concentrated barrage of negative criticism.'

Rakhmaninov felt that taken individually, members of the audience would be poor critics of music; but as a complete body, the audience never errs! Contrary to the dire predictions that his music would be irrelevant and forgotten in a generation, it has been the critics and their tirades that have dimmed in memory, leaving Rakhmaninov's music unfettered by stigma and free for exploration and regeneration. In the words of Claudio Arrau, 'Rakhmaninov was one of the few musicians worthy of immortality.'

As for Rakhmaninov's reply to Downes: *Yes I do. I believe that it is possible to be serious, to have something to say to people while yet remaining popular. I believe that. But others do not. They think as you do.*

AARON SHORR

Origins (1873–1897)

Sergey Vassilievich Rakhmaninov was born on 20 March 1873 in Semyonovo, one of his parents' estates in the Staraya Russa region to the south of Lake Ilmen. No description of the exact position and appearance of the estate survives. The family came from old Russian aristocratic roots which could be traced back to the 15th century but family records mention no one of particular distinc-
tion; the Rakhmaninovs never moved in the higher echelons of the nobility. From the early 18th century they had lived on their country estates in the Tambov region. According to family tradition the composer's father, Vassily Arkadievich (1841–1916), served in the army as a young man, seeing action in the campaign against Jamil's Islamic resistance movement in the Caucasus from 1857 to 1859. Later, serving with a hussar regi-
ment, he took part in the sup-
pression of the Polish uprising of 1863. After his marriage to a wealthy general's daughter,

Vassily Rakhmaninov

Lyubov Petrovna Butakova (1848–1929), Vassily Arkadievich resigned his commission. Had he had the expertise to manage the five estates which his wife brought as her dowry, he would have enjoyed security from then on, but instead he spent his time in social pleasures and neglected his business affairs. Like many other Russian nobles in the 19th century, he squandered his entire marriage settlement within just a few years. Soon after Sergey's birth he had to surrender Semyonovo, the last estate but one, and in 1882 the last one, Oneg, which lay on the Volga not far from Novgorod, where Sergey spent his early childhood.

The infant Rakhmaninov with his mother

Sergey was the fourth of six children. With so many siblings one might expect a wealth of childhood memories, but in fact his recollections are limited to a few brief comments, more about his impressions of the countryside and the atmosphere of old Russia than about members of his family.

His parents seem to have been a strange couple. His mother was reserved, cool and strict, sometimes even frightening, while his father was the exact opposite. '. . . *sociable, with a happy disposition and an incredible fantasist. The things he dreamt up, the number of cock-and-bull stories he told about himself and his life! . . . He never had a penny, was up to his ears in debt, but never got depressed about it . . . He was a debauched, lovable and very gifted idler.*'[1] Sergey's mother's lack of warmth and his father's engaging but negligent attitude led their son many years later to say categorically: *His parents did not love him very much.*[2] This is a strange use of the third person to express both detachment and hurt feelings. As a result of financial ruin and the forced move to St Petersburg in 1882, his parents' relationship deteriorated so much that shortly afterwards they separated permanently, thus bringing Sergey's family life to a sad and early end.

Rakhmaninov's mother, who had the care of the children, made strenuous efforts to secure their future, but the possibilities were limited by their straitened circumstances. However, she did manage to arrange for their education with relatives who put them up temporarily and in boarding schools. This may be one reason why Sergey lost sight of his siblings very early on. Considering that family ties are traditionally more highly valued in Russia than in the West, his further contacts with his family can

Irish composer and pianist, John Field (1782–1837) is credited for his innovation of the 'nocturne' piano genre, which Chopin, in turn, elevated to an exquisite art form. Field's career began with an apprenticeship to Muzio Clementi. The arrangement was difficult for Field, who suffered from Clementi's avarice. At the end of the apprenticeship, mentor and pupil went on grand a tour of Europe, playing joint concerts en route to Vienna, where Clementi hoped to deposit Field with Beethoven's teacher, Albrechtsberger. Eventually freeing himself from indentured servitude, Field made his way to Russia, where he established a reputation as pianist and teacher. Field was an important foreign influence in laying the seeds of what was later to become the 'Russian School' of piano playing. His most prominent pupil from this period was Mikhail Glinka.

only be described as sporadic. His early estrangement from his family was particularly apparent in his moments of depression: in a letter written in February 1893: *Father leads a dissolute life, mother is gravely ill, my older brother gets into debt and God only knows how it will be paid off . . . and my younger brother is terrifyingly lazy.*[3] In another context he says about him: *A person with whom it is better not to be acquainted.*[4] Though this negative attitude may have been due to some particular circumstance, it still indicates his basic relationship to his family as a whole.

Sergey's musical gifts came from his father's side. His grandfather Arkady Alexandrovich (1808–1881) was a talented amateur pianist and composer. He was a pupil of the Irish pianist, John Field. His father also played the piano enthusiastically and entertained his friends with salon pieces and improvisations. 'He played the piano for hours on end – no well-known pieces, goodness knows what they were but you could have listened to him for ever.'[5] A lot of the music, which he thought or said he had made up, he had actually picked up somewhere else – for instance the Polka V R, of which Sergey later made a virtuoso transcription in memory of his father.

Among his siblings only his older sister Yelena showed any musical inclination. She had an expressive contralto voice and sang to Sergey's accompaniment, introducing him, among other things, to Tchaikovsky's songs. Her career, which began with an engagement at the Bolshoi Theatre, was cut short by her sudden death from anaemia. The most notable musical talent in the family to date had only recently emerged in Sergey's older cousin Alexander Ziloti (1863–1945), the son of one of his father's sisters. After graduating as a pianist from the St Petersburg Conservatory, Ziloti continued his studies with Liszt in Weimar; he became known as one of the most promising Russian pianists. He was to be a helpful and energetic mentor to his younger cousin.

Sergey's mother and her family deserve much credit for encouraging him. She early recognised his exceptional musical gifts and gave him his first piano lessons. At the age of four he could already read music and soon after was playing with some skill for his age. 'One day, when Sergey was still a small boy, his grandfather Arkady Alexandrovich came to Oneg and sat down with his grandson to play a Beethoven sonata arranged for four hands. They were engrossed in their playing and when they had finished the grandfather turned to his grandson with joy and pride. At that moment Sergey's former nurse, a peasant on the estate, came into the room to ask for straw to mend the roof of her house. "You are worth a lot more for having brought up such a grandson" the grandfather told the woman, who did not really understand why she was worth so much, if her "brought-up one" played the piano cleverly.'[6] By the age of seven music had become a vital necessity to Rakhmaninov. His sister's Swiss governess later told him: 'Do you remember the day when an excursion was arranged for some guests, how you stayed home with the pretext of not feeling well and I was obliged to stay too and take care of you? A few minutes after all had departed you came to me and in your most cajoling way asked if you could play the . . . piano . . . When I was finally persuaded to allow this, you surprised me by suggesting that I sing the song your mother liked to hear and that you would accompany me. I did not take you seriously, but you insisted and I agreed. And how astonished I was to hear your small hands play chords that may not have been complete, but were certainly without a single wrong note. You made me sing Schubert's *Plainte d'une jeune fille (Mädchenklage)* three times and I had to promise not to tell your mother how we spent the afternoon. Unfortunately – or rather, fortunately – I did not keep my word and told your mother that evening. Next morning the news was sent to your grandfather [Butakov], who . . . ordered your father to go to Petersburg and bring back a good piano teacher from the Conservatory.'[7]

Sergey had his first regular piano tuition from Anna Ornatskaya, a young graduate of the St Petersburg Conservatory, who recognised the extent of his talent. She persuaded his parents, after they gave up Oneg, that he must pursue a musical career and procured a place for him at the Conservatory. Sergey entered the bottom class to prepare for studying the piano, but also took lessons in theory and history of music and general subjects. He found it difficult to settle into his new environment; he missed the peace and calm of country life at Oneg and longed to be reunited with his parents. One of his aunts and his maternal grandmother occasionally looked after him, but after a while he began to play truant and failed in important subjects.

Looking back, he said: *My grandmother was very good; she believed everything I said. I used to get ten kopecks a day from her for my expenses and the fare to the Conservatory, but I would go straight to the skating pond and spend the whole morning there . . . I achieved a great perfection in skating and never went near the Conservatory. But I would get the hateful book with the marks. Oh, how I hated it. I would bring it home, take a candle, and go straight to the W.C. There I would lock myself in, and soon all the low marks would be changed into high ones . . . How my*

Lyubov Rakhmaninov and Anna Ornatskaya

grandmother was so easily deceived, I do not understand. One spring my book showed that I was pretty nearly at the top of our class. We went to Novgorod to spend the summer on my grandmother's estate. But this time my mother was with us. And so it was an altogether different proposition. One could not deceive her. To make things worse, one of the teachers from the Conservatory came to visit us. 'Poor Serioya,' she said. 'Why? What is the matter?' came a shower of questions. She answered: 'But don't you know? He has flunked all his general courses.' So every-

Rakhmaninov seated at the piano aged nine

thing was found out. I could manage only the music without studying.[8]

In this period his Butakov grandmother was closest to him; in her he felt a tenderness which his mother completely lacked. In the summer months she took him to the country and, being deeply devout, visited local monasteries and churches in the area with the boy, giving him a lasting impression of the Eastern Orthodox liturgy and, particularly, the sound of bells.

Because he had done so badly in general subjects, the Conservatory threatened to expel him in the spring of 1885. His mother was in despair but behaved sensibly and asked Alexander Ziloti for advice. Once he had heard Sergey play the piano he advised her to send the boy to Moscow to study with his own former teacher, the famous piano professor Nikolay Sergeyevich Zverev (1832–1893), who specialised in training young pianists.

Throughout Rakhmaninov's music, the influence of bells was a constant, whether in the choral symphony, The Bells, the finale of the First Suite for Two Pianos, the opening of the Second Piano Concerto or the op 39 Études-Tableaux. Rakhmaninov reminisced, The sound of church bells dominated all the cities of Russia I used to know – Novogorod, Kiev, Moscow. They accompanied every Russian from childhood to the grave, and no composer could escape their influence.

In the autumn of 1885 Zverev accepted the twelve-year old Rakhmaninov into his class at the Moscow Conservatory, took him into his house and undertook to educate him. Zverev, an outstanding teacher, set great store by a broad general education, as well as specialised instruction for pianists. He had two or three talented pupils staying with him at any one time, so that he could concentrate on their education and training. Rakhmaninov and his fellow pupils Maximov and Presman benefited from his intuitive empathy with his charges and utter single-mindedness. Matvey Presman's recollections of his tutelage in Zverev's house offer some interesting insights. Zverev's training revolved around practising the piano for several hours a day under his strict supervision. 'There was absolute order during our lessons. Since all three of us had to play . . . we had to stick to a prearranged timetable . . . Twice a week each of us had to get up earlier than the others in order to start playing at six in the morning.'[9]

Zverev demanded neither living expenses nor fees from his pupils; on the contrary, being a supreme idealist, he placed so much value on putting his ideas on teaching into practice that he treated his pupils with exceptional generosity. For him their success was recognition and justification enough: 'Meanwhile he spent his colossal fortune on us. Living at Zverev's we did not pay anything for accommodation or for food. Most of all, he took upon himself to provide for all our clothing requirements; he paid for tutors in all the subjects of a normal education and in French and German as well.'[10]

Wherever possible Zverev encouraged his students' artistic interests, trying to awaken their appreciation and develop their

Nikolay Zverev sits at the centre of his class of 1888, Rakhmaninov stands behind him, Alexander Scriabin is seated on the left

taste; he took them to plays, ballets, operas and concerts. 'As a consequence of his enormous dedication Zverev never paid any attention to the amount of time he devoted to his pupils. In all the years that I stayed in the class with Zverev I never once went home during the summer holidays to visit my family. During the summer we would all go to the dacha outside Moscow . . . or once to the Crimea. Zverev always brought a piano with him to the dacha so that he could give us lessons and as a result expected us to work just as hard during the summer as we did in the winter. Something that has remained particularly memorable for me is the trip to the Crimea where we stayed with friends of Zverev's and . . . a teacher from the Conservatory came too to give us theory lessons.'[11]

Zverev regarded preparing his pupils for public performance and getting them used to it as an integral part of their training; he let them take part in student recitals at an early stage. Even Sergey, while he was still among the youngest in his class, often

The influence of Anton Rubinstein's (1829–1894) career can be compared in magnitude to that of Liszt. A pupil of Alexandre Villoing (1804–1878), who was in turn the pupil of John Field's student, Dubuc, Rubinstein had a dazzling career as a child prodigy, touring Europe to great acclaim. In maturity, Rubinstein combined educational aspects with his recitals, offering fascinating overviews and commentary on the great breadth of piano literature. These 'historical' concerts had a profound impact on the emerging generation of Russian artists, including the young, enthralled Rakhmaninov. He would later recount, *I had the great good fortune to attend Rubinstein's historical concerts. He would come out on the platform and merely say: "Every note of Chopin's is pure gold. Listen." And then he played and we listened!*

In 1862, Rubinstein became the director of the new St Petersburg Conservatory, a post he held for five years – resuming the same position in 1887 for another four years.

played at the Conservatory, where both Tchaikovsky (1840–1893) and Anton Rubinstein (1829–1894), the famous pianist, composer and founder of Russian musical education, were among the audience. He was immediately noticed. One of Zverev's maxims was to distrust public applause and he therefore rarely expressed satisfaction with his pupils, merely acknowledging rather than praising them. However, in the presence of other people he did praise their achievements to spur them on. Rakhmaninov's recollections of Sunday concerts in Zverev's house are illuminating. *Zverev turned his home from what might have been a musical prison into a musical paradise. From a very strict teacher, he completely changed on Sundays. That afternoon and evening he always kept open house for the greatest figures in the Moscow musical world. Tchaikovsky, Taneyev, Arensky, Safonov, Ziloti, as well as university professors, lawyers, actors, would drop in, and the hours passed in talk and music. For us boys the delightful feature of these Sundays was that Zverev would not permit any of the great musicians present to touch the piano, unless by way of some explanation or criticism. For we, not they, were the solo artists on these occasions. Our impromptu performances were Zverev's greatest joy. No matter what we played, his verdict was always 'Fine! Well done! Excellent!' He let us play anything we felt like playing, and would call on his guests to bear him out in his opinion of us.*[12]

At the beginning of 1886 Anton Rubinstein mounted the first series of his Moscow Historical Concerts, which left a lasting impression on Rakhmaninov, for whom Rubinstein became the absolute ideal of piano playing. *He sat at the piano and played and explained. He included all the important composers from the oldest classics down to his own day, and the Russian School . . . He played everything inimitably.*[13]

In 1888 Rakhmaninov started in Ziloti's advanced piano class. He would have preferred to attend Vassily Safonov's lessons (Zverev's famous pupil Alexander Scriabin changed over to him), but that was not Zverev's intention and as Rakhmaninov was still living with him he felt bound to follow his wishes. He first had to pass a test in which his brilliant piano technique was conspicuous. Tchaikovsky, the chairman of the examiners, was enthusiastic and gave Rakhmaninov a special distinction.

Upon changing to Ziloti's class, Rakhmaninov also started studying counterpoint with Sergey Taneyev (1856–1915), plus fugue and free composition with Anton Arensky (1861–1906). Composing fulfilled his deepest needs. He had already secretly made some attempts in the summer of 1887 and had only let Presman know about it. 'He became very pensive, even gloomy, seeking out solitude, pacing about with his head hung low, his gaze straining towards some point in space. Moreover he would mutter things under his breath, waving his hands as if he were conducting. This state of mind lasted a few days. Finally, choosing a moment when no-one apart from me was around, with an air of mystery he beckoned me toward the piano and began to play. Having finished playing he asked me: *Do you know what that is?* 'No', I said, 'I don't.' *And how do you like the pedal point in the bass under the chromatic scales in the upper part?* Having received a satisfactory response he said, rather pleased with himself: *I composed it myself and I dedicate the piece to you.*[14]

During the years with Zverev, Rakhmaninov had greatly changed: he was now introverted and controlled to a degree unusual at his age and had lost the last vestiges of childish playfulness. He attacked his composition studies with great eagerness and here too outstripped his fellow students, but far from becoming a loner, he was always helpful and friendly to them.

At the beginning of 1889 Rakhmaninov and Zverev parted company. Presman reports: 'When Rakhmaninov left, Zverev took it very badly. The horrendous scene that accompanied their discussion and parting is forever engraved in my memory; it turned out to be a very serious matter. Zverev was upset almost to the point of losing his mind. He considered himself insulted and no arguments of Rakhmaninov's could change his mind. Only someone of Rakhmaninov's stoicism could have borne that scene. The essential and the one and only reason for him to move on from Zverev's was the utter impossibility of studying composition there. During the course of the day the playing of the grand piano did not cease in Zverev's flat. Admittedly all three of us did have to play but to compose while someone was playing in the next room was of course impossible for him. Zverev did not want to understand this; he was so offended, or rather considered himself so insulted by Rakhmaninov, that he broke off all contact with him.'[15]

In the last analysis it is hard to say what caused Zverev to take offence. Was it Rakhmaninov's high-handedness in preferring composition to the piano in defiance of his teacher's ideas, or was there bad blood among the pupils, as his cousin Sophia Satina maintained, because Zverev always favoured the more gifted Rakhmaninov?[16] Perhaps there were several struggles going on simultaneously. What ultimately precipitated the rift is unknown.

Fortunately, Varvara Arkadievna Satina, a sister of his

Alexander Ziloti (1863–1945) was a pivotal figure in Russian musical history. As a student of Nikolay and Anton Rubinstein, Liszt, Tchaikovsky and Zverev, Ziloti's career, like Rakhmaninov's, effortlessly spanned the disciplines of pianist, composer, conductor and teacher. He was a significant promoter of new music and his St Petersburg concert series boldly featured the premieres of works by Delius, Elgar, Stravinsky, Prokofiev, Debussy, Sibelius and Scriabin. Diaghilev first encountered Stravinsky's music at one of Ziloti's concerts. At Ziloti's behest, Rakhmaninov aired the 2nd and 3rd movements of his new and as yet unfinished C minor Piano Concerto, with Ziloti also making his conducting debut. The subsequent success of this performance lifted Rakhmaninov's spirits and heralded a new period of creative success after the dreaded failure of his First Symphony.

Rakhmaninov sitting with the Skalon sisters at the Ignatov estate in 1897

father's who lived in Moscow, took in the young man, who would otherwise have been left without money or lodgings. She gave him a room in her house where he could study undisturbed. Her sons and daughters were about the same age as him (including the girl he was to marry) and welcomed him kindly. He soon felt completely at home among them.

Rakhmaninov spent the summer of 1890 and many summers thereafter with the Satin family at Ivanovka, their country estate in Tambov province about 500 kilometres southwest of Moscow. This eventually became his property. It is now a Rakhmaninov museum. *I grew fond of this landscape and, away from it, would find myself longing for it, for Ivanovka offered the repose of surrounding that hard work requires – at least, for me. There were none of the beauties of nature that are usually thought of in this term – no mountains, precipice or winding shore. This steppe was like an infinite sea where the waters are actually boundless fields of wheat, rye, oats, stretching from horizon to horizon. Sea air is often praised, but how much more do I love the air of the steppe, with its aroma of earth and all that grows and blossoms.*[17]

In the summer of 1890 distant relatives of the Satins were staying at Ivanovka, among them the daughters of General Skalon. Rakhmaninov was particularly attracted to Vera, the youngest of the three, and fell deeply in love with her, but her parents considered this youthful romance socially unacceptable and forbade any contact between them. He even had to send letters via her sisters. Before her marriage to an officer in 1899 'she burnt more than a hundred letters from Seriozha [Sergey] . . . to the day she died she did not forget or stop loving Seriozha'[18] one of her sisters later recalled.

When Alexander Ziloti announced his resignation from the teaching staff of the Moscow Conservatory in protest against the dictatorial Vassily Safonov's appointment as director, Rakhmaninov strove to complete his piano studies forthwith, so as not to have to change teachers. As there was no doubt about his ability, he was allowed to sit his examination early, in May 1891. Once again he was able to demonstrate his supreme pianism in the set programme, which consisted of Beethoven's Waldstein Sonata op 53, Chopin's B-flat minor Sonata op 35 and some smaller pieces. He duly received his piano diploma.

In that same year he also produced a mature composition: his First Piano Concerto in F-sharp minor, completed during the summer at Ivanovka. In March 1892 he played the first movement in a Conservatory concert, accompanied by the student orchestra under Safonov. A young music student, Alexander Osovsky, described the impression it made on him: 'I remember the whole concert hall being roused by the impassioned, thunderous explosion with which, after two bars in unison from the orchestra, Rakhmaninov savagely fell upon the keyboard in fast descending octaves at a magnificent *fortissimo*. Having once gained mastery of the audience, he held its attention in a state of unrelenting suspense through to the very end of the performance. Regardless of the fact that this concerto was his first opus, before us stood an artist of immense originality. Perhaps at particular moments a hint of Tchaikovsky glimmers through some passages, but the work's monumental nature, the sweep, the dramatic tension, the impassioned pathos, the captivating, melodious lyricism, the commanding force of the rhythm, the shape of the melodic and harmonic ideas all pointed to the untrodden paths down which he was already travelling . . .'[19]

That month Rakhmaninov also took his final composition examination. He was required to write a one-act opera *Aleko*, based on Pushkin's poem *The Gypsies*. Rakhmaninov was fascinated with the subject matter and went to work with a will. In an incredibly short time – less than three weeks – he had almost completed the hour-long score. When he played it on the piano to the examination board the members were so enthusiastic that they awarded him the Great Gold Medal – an honour which had only been bestowed twice before in the history of the Conservatory. To Rakhmaninov's joy even Zverev congratulated him on his success, thus paving the way for the reconciliation he had long hoped for. From then on their relationship remained warm and untroubled until Zverev's death in 1893.

Aleko established Rakhmaninov as an experienced composer, which also buoyed up his finances, as the work was accepted for the following season in Moscow and the publisher Gutheil bought the score for a generous sum.

Aleko is the first of Rakhmaninov's works to be generally recognised but it never became established in the Russian operatic repertory. The plot unfolds in the course of one night. Aleko, a romantic fugitive from civilisation, has found refuge among the gypsies, impressed by their carefree lifestyle. He is living with Semfira, a young gypsy girl whose father warns him that her mother had left him for another man but that as a gypsy who respects the freedom of his fellows he had been prepared to accept her decision. The same fate awaits Aleko. Semfira's feelings towards him have cooled and she has fallen in love with a young man from her tribe. When Aleko catches the lovers red-handed he loses control and kills them, whereupon the gypsies reject him, because 'we, free sons of the wild, know neither punishment nor judgment; we do not thirst for blood and tears but we do not condone a murderer.'[20]

The libretto by Vladimir Nemirovich-Danchenko, a devotee of the Italian verismo opera which was then enjoying its first successes in Russia, is modelled on Pietro Mascagni's *Cavalleria Rusticana.* The central elements of the plot – simple lifestyle, a crime of passion – and its structure as a one-act opera in two scenes connected by an orchestral interlude also follow this example. The music is authentic Rakhmaninov, even though it is influenced by Russian classical opera composers, particularly Tchaikovsky but also marginally Borodin and Rimsky-Korsakov. The plot lacks inner cohesion, due to weaknesses in the libretto and under-characterised singing parts, which follow each other with little dramatic motivation even though they are exquisitely lyrical. To please contemporary taste Rakhmaninov wrote exotic songs and dances for the gypsies. For long periods the orchestra only provides a background and sets the mood but when the opportunity occurs, as for example in the Interlude, it speaks with an independent voice. The best-known number is Aleko's cavatina at the end of the first scene in which he sings of his love for Semfira – an aria inextricably associated with the name of Fyodor Chaliapin, who from 1897 on made it one of his signature tunes.

In the spring of 1893 the Bolshoi Theatre finally presented the premiere of *Aleko.* The enormous acclaim from press and public brought Rakhmaninov outside invitations, including one to conduct the opera in Kiev. The critic Semyon Kruglikov wrote: 'Rakhmaninov is a talented man, well versed and with excellent taste. He might become a good opera composer, because he has a feel for the stage. He has an almost infallible understanding of the human voice and is endowed with the lucky gift of the melodist . . . Not one of all our best composers made his debut at such an early age with an opera of the quality of *Aleko*.'[21]

In spite of this appreciation the composer had no good words for the work in later years and thought it not Russian enough. He said: *It is written on the old-fashioned Italian model, which Russian composers, in most cases, have been accustomed to follow,*[22] and so inevitably he categorically refused Chaliapin's request in 1937 to make a fundamental revision of the work.

Rakhmaninov was dismissive about his Piano Trio op 9. On one occasion he bumped into David Schor, pianist of the Moscow Trio, who was scheduled to perform it. Rakhmaninov admonished him for programming this trio, which he disliked intensely. Schor defended the trio and invited Rakhmaninov to their dress rehearsal. Rakhmaninov attended the rehearsal and made many interpretative suggestions, cuts and even composed several new bars for inclusion. After hearing their performance, Rakhmaninov exclaimed, *You have made me love my trio. Now I will play it!*

In the summer of 1893 Rakhmaninov completed a Fantasy for Two Pianos op 5, dedicated to Tchaikovsky, and the symphonic poem *The Cliff* op 7. When Tchaikovsky heard of this copious output he rejoined jokingly that he himself had only completed a little symphony that summer (his famous 6th Symphony, the *Pathétique*) but he gladly accepted Rakhmaninov's invitation to a performance of the Fantasy planned for the autumn. He was fated not to attend the concert, as he died in October of that year.

Tchaikovsky had always treated Rakhmaninov generously and was complimentary about the young composer. He showed his interest in the Piano Pieces op 3 and according to reliable sources he encouraged the generally favourable reviews which declared the works on the whole promising and in some respects even masterly.

Pyotr Tchaikovsky by Kusnetsov, 1893

Tchaikovsky's death came as a serious blow to Rakhmaninov. In his sorrow he wrote his Piano Trio op 9, the Trio Élégiaque 'dedicated to the memory of a great artist', just as Tchaikovsky had dedicated his Piano Trio op 50 to the memory of Nikolay Rubinstein (1835–1881), the brother of Anton and founder of the Moscow Conservatory.

The demands and musical resources of the Trio in D minor make it Rakhmaninov's most important youthful work. Its sweeping grandeur and emotional power prefigure three later works in the same turbulent key: the First Symphony of 1895, the First Piano Concerto of 1907 and the Third Piano Concerto of 1909. In the Trio the piano is given not just a dominant but a virtuoso role – entirely in keeping with the genre of chamber music – which shows that the composer intended to follow that tradition and to emulate Tchaikovsky's Trio, which he does to the point of adopting a similar sequence of movements and alluding to it both in thematic material and in the detailed process of its development. As in Tchaikovsky's work, the first movement (marked *moderato*) is the core of the Trio and is based on a broadly constructed sonata form. Repeated falling chromatic scales supporting delicate, swirling motifs above them set the prevailing mood, while the second subject and the final theme are more energetic and build up quickly to an emotional climax. The development section is mainly based on the concise motifs of the opening, out of which Rakhmaninov draws a rich variety of harmony and rhythm. The *quasi variazioni* second movement is a series of variations on a melancholy, pastoral theme. The detachment indicated by the word 'quasi' is justified by a moment of free improvisation, on which Rakhmaninov based much of the abundant variety of invention that follows. The finale, marked *allegro risoluto*, is by comparison more concentrated and intensely, passionately expressive. The work ends with a sad and agitated epilogue which revisits the dynamic main theme of the first movement and so brings the work full circle, as the strains of the opening passage gradually die away.

For all the respect the Trio deserves, it is not without its weaknesses. On hearing a later performance, Taneyev remarked in terms which harshly pointed out the technical shortcomings of the work: '. . . the Trio shows talent, but is a formless, pointless essay in modulations, is bereft of themes and endlessly repeats one and the same thing . . .'[23]

The composer himself was unhappy with the work and when he first revised it in 1907 he made several cuts, simplified the piano part and in the middle movement rewrote the solo piano variation (no 6) for the whole ensemble. Ten years later he cut away some more of the detail, but these alterations were not incorporated into the score until the Moscow edition of 1950.

When Rakhmaninov first started to earn money, he was tempted to adopt an extravagant lifestyle which inevitably led him into difficulties. His cousin Sophia Satina remembers him at that time: 'He was young, loved to play the dandy, to drive about in a smart carriage and to throw his money around. He wanted a life with fewer responsibilities but the wage he earned from composing, although Gutheil assiduously bought everything he wrote, was not enough for the life he led. Nevertheless, he frequently started feeling tormented by the thought that he would have to write something successful and would get a grip of himself just in time to earn some money.' [24]

Constant financial worries drove Rakhmaninov to giving private tuition, but he did so reluctantly. He thought teaching a complete waste of time and was inclined to postpone or cancel lessons. He was virtually at a loss when his pupils played to him, because all he could do was to confront their earnest desire to improve with his own faultless technique. Clearly he was not a good teacher and teaching was an obstacle to his phenomenal gifts as pianist and composer. From 1894 he worked in various establishments, teaching among other subjects elementary musical theory. One of his girl students recalls: 'Teaching really disrupted his creative work. Therefore his negative attitude to his classes is quite understandable. And he did not disguise the fact; his physical demeanour and the way he held himself made it quite clear.' [25] He was fortunate in his superiors, who did everything they could to keep his commitments to a minimum; in his last years in Moscow his 'duties' as a 'Music Inspector' were restricted to overseeing examinations and recitals.

In the autumn of 1895 Rakhmaninov embarked on his first extensive concert tour, as duet partner to the violinist Teresina Tua. This was supposed to last for three months, with performances in a large number of Russian cities, but it ended earlier than anyone concerned had expected. Rakhmaninov thoroughly disliked travelling and found long journeys in coaches particularly wearisome, so he made an excuse about a delayed payment from his agent and without warning returned to Moscow. On the way, to his surprise, he met the promoter of the tour, who made no fuss about it and released the unnerved musician from his distasteful obligations.

Rakhmaninov's First Symphony in D minor – on which he lavished a great deal of time and effort and had high hopes – was not destined for success. The premiere in St Petersburg on 15 May 1897 under the baton of Alexander Glazunov was icily rejected. César Cui, one of the group of St Petersburg composers known as the 'mighty handful', also known for his frequently vitriolic reviews, wrote that he had heard a work which made him think of a symphony on the theme of the Seven Plagues of Egypt. This symphony might well have been more kindly received in Moscow. One explanation of the indifference and lack of interest which it encountered in St Petersburg was the latent antagonism between the two rival musical capitals of Russia. At the premiere Glazunov did not seem appropriately enthusiastic: 'He stood phlegmatically on the podium and just as phlegmatically conducted the symphony.'[26]

Rakhmaninov brooded deeply over this failure. He tried to explain the work's lack of success by assuming it was due to its shortcomings. The score, which he had already delivered to Gutheil, was withdrawn at his express wish and not published.

In later years he still could not make up his mind to publish it. Twenty years after the premiere he wrote to the musicologist Boris Asafyev: *Good things repeatedly failed to hit the mark; it was the bad ones which were popular. Before the symphony was performed I had an excessively high opinion of it but after the first run-through my views changed radically. Really what still comes back to me now is the middle of it. Somewhere in it there is some not too bad music, but there is a lot more that is weak, childish, forced and bombastic . . . It is very badly orchestrated and was equally badly performed (Glazunov was the conductor). After this symphony I did not write anything for about three years; I was like a man who had suffered a blow which paralysed his head and hands for a long time.*[27]

Moscow a view of the Kremlin at the turn of the 19th Century

A survey of the works Rakhmaninov wrote before 1897 reveals the development of a growing artistic personality, with an individual style and means of expression. Tchaikovsky's influence on him is always, and rightly, emphasised and as a student under Arensky and Taneyev at the Moscow Conservatory (both declared admirers of Tchaikovsky) he could hardly escape it. Yet this influence applies less to the actual technical details of composition than to a general level of creative insight – the concept of music as an art which expresses emotion, as a personal statement – and from this springs his inclination towards sensuous lyricism. In the very works in which Rakhmaninov explicitly alludes to Tchaikovsky, such as the Trio Élégiaque op 9, he is far from a poor imitation of the master. The power of his thematic invention and his broad arching melodies, especially in the first movement, bear witness to a wholly independent creativity.

Rakhmaninov wrote his piano works under the influence of Chopin and Liszt, the two most important and historically significant composers for that instrument in the late 19th century, partly, of course, because they had already been accepted in Russian piano music. Through Ziloti, who was one of the keenest propagandists and devotees of Liszt in Russia, he came into contact with the finesse of his piano writing and his musical innovations. In the early piano works, however, the influence of Chopin is paramount. One instance is the classically concentrated form, characteristic pianistic technique and choice of typical Chopinesque titles (*Nocturne, Waltz, Barcarolle, Mazurka*) in the Morceaux de Salon op 10. Rakhmaninov's success in emulating Chopin's nobility of style had its limitations, however. The latter's depiction of an aristocratic Paris salon has an authentic ring, whereas Rakhmaninov's seems second-hand and turns into a bourgeois drawing-room. In the Moments Musicaux op 16, Rakhmaninov's first outstanding piano work, all the typical elements of his style are clearly present – elegant passage-work and figuration, complete sureness of touch, richness of tone and strong harmonic foundation in the bass line.

The First Piano Concerto is in many respects less reminiscent of Chopin, Liszt or Russian models than of Grieg's A minor Concerto op 16, which the composer learned when studying with Ziloti. The soloist's effective opening cascade of octaves, the elegiac first theme, the expansive cadenza at the end of the first movement – are all enough to indicate that he took the Grieg Concerto as his model. The pianistic structure of this First Concerto is also reminiscent of Grieg, particularly in its original version though less so in the generally known revision of 1917, in which the composer tautened the overall design and also refined the piano part in line with his later experience.

Rakhmaninov's training under Arensky and Taneyev at the Moscow Conservatory was thorough, but even for that period decidedly conservative. Both teachers followed Tchaikovsky's compositional principles, although with different emphasis and different results, so in that sense Rakhmaninov passed through a Tchaikovsky-style school of composition – which viewed both the 'New German school' of Liszt and Wagner and contemporary French composers with similar scepticism. Composers such as Wagner or Debussy, to whose works students should really have been applying themselves, were not on the syllabus. Such basic study might have left a powerful imprint on Rakhmaninov's development, for although he was not unreceptive to contemporary music he was little drawn to emulate the musical innovations of his day. His studies strengthened this attitude, in contrast to other composers who felt a much stronger impetus to go down that road, precisely because the moderns had been withheld from them in their student days.

His training followed a particular Germanic model, as the Rubinstein brothers, who founded the Moscow and St Petersburg Conservatories, were both German-trained. It was this Austro-Germanic contrapuntal tradition which Taneyev imparted most enduringly to Rakhmaninov. With him he studied the strict (Palestrina) style of counterpoint – a discipline which did not initially attract him but eventually awakened his interest, thanks to his teacher's motivation. Above all, however, he learnt to appreciate Taneyev's masterly musical understanding and unchallenged critical judgement. After he left the Conservatory he kept in contact with him, sought his advice and showed him his latest works before presenting them before the public.

Arensky exerted an equal influence on Rakhmaninov, although perhaps the younger man did not take his teacher's compositions as seriously as they warranted. Arensky's music is elegant in expression, clear in form and inclined towards certain elegiac

Graduates of Anton Arensky's (standing) class from the Moscow Conservatory;
Georgy Konyus, Nikita Morosov and Rakhmaninov, seated on the right

moods – elements which had a deep impact on his young student. In his harmonies Arensky sought out new, original effects, albeit within somewhat narrow boundaries, occasionally experimenting with unconventional rhythms and metres. For Rakhmaninov these achievements were perhaps of only transitory importance, unlike the fascination they aroused in his fellow student Alexander Scriabin, whose progressive-mindedness soon led him to fall out with Arensky. Strangely enough, Rakhmaninov has left us few memories of his teacher; only once, almost casually, did he mention that he had found his harmony classes useful.[28] His personal relations with him were obviously just based on a detached, friendly respect, possibly because Arensky found teaching irksome. He insisted on keeping his distance and avoided taking any initiative, even on behalf of his most talented students.

Among his compositions Arensky wrote several suites for two pianos – a genre which impressed Rakhmaninov and on which he evidently based his Suites op 5 and op 17. The first of these, the Fantaisie-Tableaux, was his first programmatic work in the narrowest sense – a forerunner of the later Études-Tableaux op 33 and op 39. Each of the four movements is headed by a quotation from a piece of Russian poetry, from which springs a musical depiction of a particular spiritual inspiration, be it of love or nature. The transformation into the quasi-pictorial description of a situation is reflected, in all four movements, in his preference for ostinato patterns: the same melodic, harmonic and rhythmic structural motifs persist, repeated or only slightly modified; this is perhaps where much of the mystery and the compelling power of Rakhmaninov's music and its intensity lies. The second Suite op 17, a more mature composition, goes further in thematic development, relationship between the movements and grand dramatic format. Yet these works are hardly comparable: while the first Suite is more like intimate chamber music, the second is on a symphonic scale, almost like a concerto.

It is all too easy to dismiss Rakhmaninov as merely a composer for the piano, which he never was. His ability to produce a great range of moods with confidence and variety is noticeable in his early orchestral works. His marked sensitivity for orchestral colour is not only reminiscent of Tchaikovsky, but also of Rimsky-Korsakov and Arensky, who had been Tchaikovsky's pupil. The tone colours of the gypsy music in *Aleko* and in the Capriccio on Gypsy Themes op 12 never sound artificial or even forced. Among the Songs of op 4, op 8 and op 14 the restrained numbers are particularly captivating: in them Rakhmaninov succeeds in illustrating the poetic material with a sure feeling for mood. In both the vocal parts and the piano accompaniment the influence of Arensky is clearly audible. Admittedly, the poetry reflects contemporary taste but the quality of much of it is questionable today. Nevertheless, this does not detract from the standard of the songs, because the texts primarily serve as a stimulus for musical transformation, which gives them a completely fresh impact.

Maturing (1898–1908)

Artistic success not only requires genius and labour but also self-confidence and trust in one's own creative powers, of which Rakhmaninov had all too little. At regular intervals he was overwhelmed by attacks of melancholy which developed into severe bouts of depression. The debacle of the First Symphony was a catalyst, but not the cause, of a mental crisis which had been approaching for some time. Four years before, when he was barely 20 years old, he wrote to Natalya Skalon: *My spirit has aged somehow, I am tired and sometimes everything seems dreadfully unbearable. At some point I am going to crack my head in two. Every day I have fits as well and hysterics, which usually end in convulsions with my face and*

Rakhmaninov in 1897

hands twisted to the last degree . . . Is it really possible to cure moral decay? Is it really possible to reform the whole nervous system? Incidentally I tried to do it for several nights by binges and getting drunk. But that did not help and I gave up, i.e. I decided to stop drinking like that altogether. It doesn't help and it isn't necessary. People often tell me . . . 'Stop getting depressed. At your age and with your talents it's simply criminal.' But they always forget that apart from being (perhaps) a gifted musician . . . I am a human being like everyone else, expecting out of life what everyone else expects . . . But what is more I, with the state of affairs as they are (oh, this state of affairs!) am an unfortunate human being and as a human being I shall never be happy, because of my character. This last I prophesy for myself in the sober conviction that it will turn out to be so.[29]

Never in his life did his contemporaries find Rakhmaninov a carefree or happy person. He struggled with himself and his temperament and endured constant mood swings, which made life difficult for him. As the years went by he learned to live with his bouts of depression and to control the outward symptoms. Without speculating as to the causes of this depression, it is interesting to consider whether and in what way it affected his creative work. It certainly does seem as though something gloomy and brooding often speaks through his music. The works themselves give out clues: dark timbres, a preference for minor keys and drawn-out tempi, insistence on rhythmic formality and delicate, recurring motifs.

Music must come from the heart and go to the heart . . . Composing is as essential a part of my being as breathing or eating; it is one of the necessary functions of living . . . What I try to do, when writing down my music, is to make it say simply and directly that which is in my heart when I am composing. If there is love there, or bitterness, or sadness, or religion, these moods become a part of my music.

Rakhmaninov in an interview with *The Étude*, Philadelphia, Dec 1941.

A certain scepticism is necessary when reading artists' views of themselves. Rakhmaninov spoke reluctantly about his work, mostly when pressed by journalists. Much of what he said sounds naïve, almost crude, but he was always sincere and honest and never thought about how his words might be interpreted. What he represents is the aesthetic principle of direct feeling; his music springs from personal emotion, independent of artistic fashion and trends, and conveys this quality to the listener. If such an aesthetic seems antiquated in the light of the radical artistic changes which took place in the 20th century, in his case it must be taken seriously. If his music does actually realise its creator's intention – direct expression of what 'fills the heart' – then it must reflect his gloominess, use it as inspiration and also convey his supremacy over it.

In the year when his First Symphony met with failure, Rakhmaninov was offered a position as conductor at the Moscow Russian Private Opera. Having long been interested in conducting, he accepted. Finance and management was in the hands of Sava Mamontov (1841–1918), a patron of the arts and an industrialist who had accumulated great wealth building railways in southern Russia.

Mamontov played an important part in late 19th-century Russian culture. He had found an artists' colony at Abramtsevo near Moscow. There he gathered around him painters, theatrical designers and sculptors (among them Valentin Serov, Mikhail Vrubel and Konstantin Korovin) and encouraged them to collaborate. He himself was particularly keen on the stage, wrote plays and enthusiastically acted in them. In the 1880s, driven by his vision of collaboration among the arts, he had created his own opera company, the Mamontov Opera, which was distinguished by the pleasure it took in bold experimentation. It gave precedence to the Russian repertory (unusual at the time), unconventional productions and sets were encouraged and talented but inexperienced musicians brought into the ensemble. Mamontov had a flair for spotting artistic talent; he discovered the famous baritone Fyodor Chaliapin (1873–1938), who would become one of Rakhmaninov's closest and most faithful friends.

Rakhmaninov was meant to make his debut with Glinka's *A Life for the Tsar*, but things went very wrong from the first rehearsal. Being inexperienced in directing an opera ensemble, he failed to give the singers their cues, so that they fell completely out of time with the orchestra. The chief conductor gleefully took over the performance; he had recognised Rakhmaninov's talent and was afraid of competition from him. The latter, however, learned his lesson quickly, and shortly afterwards won general approval with his conducting of *Samson et Dalila* by Saint-Saëns. One critic wrote: 'Rakhmaninov took the reins of the orchestra firmly and decisively in his hands and did not delay in showing what a wealth of skill as a conductor was hidden inside him. . . . Under him the orchestra sounded quite peculiar: pliable, not drowning the voices but at the same time paying a subtle attention to detail, as though this were symphonic music and not the accompaniment to an opera. Rakhmaninov's greatest merit lay in his ability to improve the sonority of the Private Opera orchestra out of all recognition.'[30]

In the following months he conducted several more well-received performances, including Dargomyzhsky's *Rusalka*, Rimsky-Korsakov's *May Night* and Bizet's *Carmen*, but intrigues and the demands of collaborating with other people in the opera house frayed his nerves. He was particularly upset by Mamontov's lack of desire to strive for perfection and the negligence with which he addressed the practical details of mounting a musical production. He therefore decided to give up his work at the Private Opera after only one year.

Besides giving him invaluable experience as a conductor, Rakhmaninov's year with Mamontov also laid the foundations for his lifelong friendship with Chaliapin. Although utterly different in character, these two artists quickly formed a close personal relationship during rehearsals. In the summer break of 1898 Rakhmaninov studied the score of *Boris Godunov* with Chaliapin and gave the naturally gifted but self-taught singer lessons in theory and history of music. In return Chaliapin enraptured Rakhmaninov with his risqué jokes and inexhaustible fund of extravagant anecdotes. The composer was enjoying life as he had not done for a long time and even began to lay plans for writing an opera. In September 1898 the two friends went on a tour

Born in the same year as Rakhmaninov, Fyodor Chaliapin (1873–1938) was the greatest operatic bass to emerge from Russia in the 20th century. His dramatic absorption in the roles he pioneered left an indelible impression on all who worked with him and experienced his genius. He was also the main inspiration for the development of Stanislavsky's method of acting. The profound friendship that existed between Rakhmaninov and Chaliapin began when the two worked together at the Mamontov Private Opera in Moscow. Chaliapin was a larger than life character – always acting, a brilliant raconteur, teeming with boundless energy and humour. The contrast with Rakhmaninov's lugubrious and laconic manner was striking and curiously beneficial to both artists. Rakhmaninov wrote of Chaliapin, *In*

the past forty-one years, from almost the very beginning of his career, of which I was witness, he quickly ascended to a pedestal from which he never descended, never slipped, till the end of his days. All concurred in the worship of his talent – ordinary people as well as the great . . .

through the south of Russia with the Mamontov Opera ensemble.

According to a later account, Anton Chekhov (1860–1904) visited them in their dressing room after a lieder recital in Yalta. Apparently he turned straight to Rakhmaninov and said: 'I have been watching you all the time, young man. You have a remarkable face – one day you are going to be a great man.'[31] These words impressed themselves on him: *To the day I die I shall remember this moment with proud satisfaction.*[32] Soon after this he sent his favourite author a score of the Symphonic Fantasy *The Cliff* with a dedication. In the spring of 1900 he met Chekhov in Yalta on several occasions, but presumably these were only brief and fleeting encounters, as we know no details about them.

Rakhmaninov's two meetings with Leo Tolstoy (1828–1910) were less successful. When he was introduced to Tolstoy soon after the fiasco of the First Symphony, the latter could find little to say,

Anton Chekhov, portrait by Josef Bvas, 1898. Tretyakov Gallery, Moscow

except to recommend him in a fatherly way to have more self-confidence and discipline in his work. Their second meeting took place in January 1900, at a time when Tolstoy was already obstinately promoting the idea of simple, natural folk art as a challenge to the established classical style. When Rakhmaninov and Chaliapin visited the Tolstoys they were asked to perform and chose Rakhmaninov's song *Fate*, which quotes Beethoven's famous 'fate' motif. *When we finished, we felt that all were delighted. Suddenly the enthusiastic applause was hushed and everyone was silent. Tolstoy sat in an armchair a little apart from the others, looking gloomy and cross. For the next hour I evaded him, but suddenly he came up to me and declared excitedly:* 'I must speak to you. I must tell you how I dislike it all!' *And he went on and on:* 'Beethoven is nonsense, Pushkin and Lermontov also.' *It was awful. Sophia Andreyevna stood behind me; she touched my shoulder and whispered:* 'Never mind, never mind. Please don't contradict him. Lyovochka must not get excited. It's very bad for him.' *After a while Tolstoy came up to me again:* 'Please excuse me. I am an old man. I did not mean to hurt you.' *I replied:* 'How could I be hurt on my own account, if I was not hurt on Beethoven's?' *But I never went back.*[33]

Strangely enough, it was just during the years of his creative crisis that Rakhmaninov's music began to be appreciated more widely – not in Russia, but in England and the USA. Alexander Ziloti had given concerts there

Rakhmaninov grew to hate the C-sharp minor Prelude op 3, no 2. It was usually called for at every one of his concert appearances. This little 'damn' prelude was his calling card to the world. Moiseiwitsch told him about a letter from a certain titled lady requesting him to perform the prelude and asking whether 'the prelude expresses the agony of a person still alive who is being nailed in his coffin?' Rakhmaninov replied, *in your place, I wouldn't try to undeceive her!* On one occasion, Rakhmaninov heard the prelude in a dance-band arrangement, which he said he preferred! Although Rakhmaninov did not secure the international copyright for this work, thereby losing an enormous fortune, he felt it opened so many doors to the musical world that he did not regret this lapse of judgement.

and included some of Rakhmaninov's music in his programmes, including the C-sharp minor Prelude op 3, no 2, which had particularly impressed the audience.

Thanks to Ziloti's contacts, Rakhmaninov was invited to London by the Philharmonic Society, apparently in an effort to introduce its subscribers to the composer of the popular Prelude. This visit to London in the spring of 1899 was the first time he had been abroad, which makes it all the more strange that we

Rakhmaninov at the Krasnyenlykoe estate of the Satin family

know nothing of his impressions at first or even second hand. The programme he offered the English public included his orchestral fantasy *The Cliff* and two of the Piano Pieces from op 3, concluding of course with the C-sharp minor Prelude. The English press praised the ability of conductor and pianist but were cautious in their judgment of the composer; nevertheless, he was invited back for the following season and as the First Piano Concerto was listed as the main work he must have had a 'better' concert in mind.

Meanwhile Rakhmaninov's own doubts about his creative gifts had not been allayed. All his attempts to return to intensive composing failed; in despair he tried to abandon work on the planned Second Concerto. The Satin family finally succeeded in persuading him to consult a doctor and sent him to the neurologist Dr Nikolay Dahl, who had made a name for himself in Moscow through his innovative therapeutic methods, including the use of hypnosis. We know nothing more about the treatment, which lasted from January to April 1900, but apparently Dahl managed to restore his self-confidence very quickly and to stimulate him with a new desire to return to composing.

The second and third movements of the Second Piano Concerto op 18 were completed first and he played them that autumn under Ziloti's baton. The Moscow critics praised him with one voice. Nikolay Kashkin wrote: 'His great talent has drawn attention to him, not only in Russia but also abroad. Now this talent is becoming as it were enlightened, conscious of its inner strength, and therefore alien to any sort of refinement and of the pursuit of extraordinary harmonic and instrumental effects which were remarked upon earlier. The classical clarity of form, the overarching melody, the splendour and power of the harmony oblige you to call this work marvellous in the full sense of the word.'[34] The missing first movement then flowed from his pen and on 27 October of the following year the first complete performance took place with the composer as soloist. The concerto, which Rakhmaninov had dedicated to Dahl in gratitude, became a great success and was enthusiastically acclaimed by the public.

The very popularity of the Second Piano Concerto today can easily lead one to lose sight of the idiosyncrasies which were once its characteristics. The very opening is unusual: a series of chords and bell-like bass notes from the soloist grow from *piano* to *fortissimo* and then the piano retreats into the background and accompanies the orchestra as it announces the main theme. Taneyev noted in his diary: 'Rakhmaninov's [Second] Concerto grows on me every time I hear it although I could cavil at the fact that the piano hardly ever plays without the orchestra.'[35] The piano is in fact largely integrated with the orchestra and rather than contending with it, performs as one among many instruments – *primus inter pares*. The composer deliberately avoided repeating the virtuoso features of the First Concerto (the soloist's opening and the cadenza), but that does not mean that the Second Concerto is easier to master; on the contrary, the technical problems are actually greater and coordination with the orchestra is more difficult. Vocal, melodic lines again predominate but here they seem longer and more fluid, and the general impression of an organic, rounded, cantabile whole is enhanced by the instrumentation,

Rakhmaninov at Krasnyenlykoe with Natalya Satin, her brother Vladimir and sister Sophia

with its choice of delicately blending colours. This work shows altogether greater technical skill in the craft of composition than the First Piano Concerto and even the First Symphony (the orchestral work which preceded it). The presentation, progression and relationship of the themes are more compelling, the large scale of its formal structure clearer and the orchestral treatment more varied. Not only does the Second Piano Concerto occupy a key role in Rakhmaninov's oeuvre for biographical reasons; it is also his first genuine masterpiece, which fully deserved a place in international concert halls.

Without the financial and psychological support of the Satin family Rakhmaninov would hardly have managed to weather the difficult years between studying at the Conservatory and the success of the Second Piano Concerto. His cousins Natalya and Sophia had taken particular trouble over him and understood and helped him during his creative crisis. Later on he referred to them as his 'doctors'.[36] He fell in love with Natalya (1877–1951), who had just graduated as a pianist from the Moscow Conservatory. Once they had overcome the objections raised by her relatives, they married in April 1902.

This step came as a complete surprise to their acquaintances and friends. 'I should say that the possibility of their marriage never crossed my mind. This was no doubt because Sergey Vassilievich never seemed to be "paying court" in his behaviour towards Natasha. It just did not in the least go with his character, his great reserve and his hatred of putting his feelings and sufferings on show. The relationship between them was like chaste friendship and companionship . . . Natasha was constantly worrying over Sergey Vassilievich's health and all the little details of everyday life which he was utterly incapable of dealing with . . . The most important thing in his life was creativity but in order for it to be fruitful those closest to him had to surround him with an atmosphere of friendship, love and concern. Family life, of which he had been deprived since he was a child, was an urgent necessity . . . It is therefore not surprising that his choice fell on Natasha; in her he of course found a faithful friend and a person who understood him perfectly.'[37]

We know little about Rakhmaninov's marriage but to all appearances it was a happy one. The couple shared their daily life together on the traditional principle of him busying himself with his work and his concert tours while Natalya Alexandrovna shielded him from mundane worries and looked after the household and children. They had two daughters – Irina, born in 1903 and Tatyana, born in 1907. Natalya, remembering him as a father, said: 'When Irina was born his joy knew no bounds, but he was so afraid of her; it seemed to him as though she somehow needed help. He kept worrying, he paced helplessly around her cradle and didn't have a clue what to do. It was just the same after the birth of our second daughter, Tanya, four years later. This touching concern about the children and his tenderness towards them lasted right until his death. He was a wonderful father. Our children adored him but were a little afraid of him – or rather, were afraid they might somehow offend or anger him. I am very proud of their love for him; for them he was the most important person in the house. At home it all revolves around what papa says and what he thinks of such and such. When the girls were grown up and Sergey Vassilievich was going out and about with them, he was quite in love with them and was proud of how good they looked.'[38]

Following the completion of the Second Piano Concerto, a Cello Sonata op 19, the Cantata *Spring* op 20 and the Songs op 21 followed in quick succession. It was as though Rakhmaninov's creative forces which had built up during the previous years were now freely pouring out.

Rakhmaninov with his dog Levko on the jetty at Krasnyenlykoe

Rakhmaninov wrote relatively little chamber music; apart from the early instrumental ensembles (the Pieces op 2 and op 6 and the posthumously published works he wrote as a student around 1890), he wrote only two great chamber works: the Trio Élégiaque op 9 and the Sonata for Cello and Piano op 19. This does not indicate a lack of interest in the classical tradition of chamber music, but as an innate melodist he avoided compositions for contrapuntal parts of equal importance, which find their most ideal realisation in classical-style string quartets. He preferred to base his compositions on a clear distinction between melody and accompaniment. With the former as his focal point, he inclined towards a monumentalisation of classical sonata form, which apparently he could only conceive of maintaining and continuing by enhancing it. This was a prerequisite for his contribution to this great tradition. Grandiloquence and conventional chamber-music style sit awkwardly together and can hardly be combined – hence his preference for symphonies and concertos and also the concerto-like features of his two major chamber works. What these compositions lack in direct intimacy can be found in the specifically chamber-music features in his songs, which broaden the traditional concept of vocal writing.

Rakhmaninov wrote the Cello Sonata for his cellist friend Anatoly Brandukov, to whom it is dedicated. This work was infused with the spirit of Chopin's Cello Sonata: it is in four movements, the cello's melodies are saturated with expressiveness and the piano has a complicated, virtuoso role to play. The first movement (*lento-allegro moderato*) begins with a slow introduction which opens out into an extended sonata form and its passionate lyricism unequivocally takes up the language of the Second Piano Concerto. The way it is enhanced and the subtle but steady intensification of the melodic lines are indebted to the earlier work. The anapaestic rhythm stated in the piano entry becomes a rhythmical leitmotif. Of the two contrasted middle movements (*allegretto scherzando* and *andante*), one is full of restlessness with lyrical passages scattered through it, while the other blossoms into a tender song which reaches emotional heights in the middle section. The finale (*allegro mosso*) is suffused with a mood of celebration, in which the sonorously flowing cello takes the lead, ignoring the importunity of the piano. A quiet coda brings peace, as the last tense outpourings are dispelled. The work is not without its problems, and successive generations of interpreters have not succeeded in displacing the impression that the composer misjudged the relative power of the two instruments.

With his Cantata *Spring*, written for baritone, mixed chorus and orchestra and set to a poem by Nikolai Nekrasov (a work little known in the West), Rakhmaninov added to the late 19th-century Russian cantata tradition, important contributions to which included Tchaikovsky's *Moscow*, Taneyev's *John of Damascus* and Rimsky-Korsakov's *Tale of Wise Oleg*. Regardless of the fact that the theme (the bursting forth of spring) was firmly rooted in Russian culture, the musical setting is less concerned with illustrative tone-painting than with the spring's impact on the human psyche. The story tells of a husband who realises that his wife has betrayed him. He resolves to kill her, but a sudden sensation of the advent of spring makes him draw back from the deed. A powerful baritone solo in operatic style – a characteristic emphasised by Chaliapin in later performances – lies at the core of the work, which prefigures the composer's two one-act operas *The Miserly Knight* and *Francesca da Rimini,* both in its style and in the colourful writing for orchestra.

In contrast to the earlier songs, in the cycle of op 21 Rakhmaninov revealed a greater refinement in painting in subtle colours, juxtaposing evocative portrayals of nature and spiritual turmoil. Best known is the fifth song, *Lilac*, for its combination of soft ostinato murmuring in the piano part with tender, dreamy cantilena. The composer later rewrote the song as a piano solo.

In the years 1902/3 the piano was once again central to Rakhmaninov's compositions. The Variations on a Theme by Chopin op 22 is his first attempt at a major piano cycle. In spite of its moments of convincing inspiration, especially in the many-faceted piano part, it is somewhat unconvincing. The work falls into attractive single sections without really seeming to be a unified cycle. Its 22 variations are inspired by Chopin's C minor Prelude op 28. Here they fall into three, more or less equal, groups. The first ten only elaborate slightly on the theme, retaining its formal structure and home key, but from variation 11 onwards the treatment is freer (key of E-flat major and slower tempo – *lento*). Through to no 18 its character moves through new keys (F minor and B-flat minor) and the original form is expanded to give the variations increasing weight and individuality. No 15 is a lively, Schumannesque scherzo with dotted rhythm, no 16 is a Chopin-style romance, and no 17 a sorrowful funeral march. The elegiac tenor of no 18 creates an epicentre of repose for the whole work. The radiant A major of no 19 marks the beginning of the final group – actually less a group than a succession of four independent character studies. No 19 is a stately overture, no 20 a brilliant concert waltz and no 21 a lyrical meditation, whose opulent glory brings the cycle to its quiet climax. A swelling virtuoso passage leads into the finale (no 22) – a surging, brilliant polonaise.

The Gutheil Edition of Rakhmaninov's Piano Works, 1900

The closing section is calm and introspective until the theme is resolved in its entirety in a pure C major.

The ten Preludes op 23 are comparable to the previous set both technically and in content and are much better known. Though forming a cycle, each prelude is self-sufficient and as a set they encompass a demanding range of moods and technical demands. The G minor (in the *alla marcia* rhythm of the outer sections) and the voluptuous D major became very popular but the flamboyant B-flat major and the intensely soulful E-flat major are equally lovely. Together with the C-sharp minor Prelude from op 3 and the later 13 Preludes op 32 Rakhmaninov covered all 24 major and minor keys, unmistakably following Chopin, but in comparison with the latter's aphoristic concision and concentration he creates grander dimensions, which allow scope for the unfolding of subtle developments and contrasts. These Preludes are actually more like mini-concertos, each striving towards large-scale effect through ornamentation and density of sound, to which they may well owe their particular charm.

In spite of his burgeoning reputation, it was still impossible for Rakhmaninov to work as an independent composer, because his fees from Gutheil and his income from occasional concerts fell far short of his needs as a breadwinner. The intrigues of the Moscow Conservatory meant that he could not expect to be offered a lucrative position as professor of piano or composition there. An invitation to join the Bolshoi Theatre as a conductor came just at the right moment. Rakhmaninov hesitated; however flattering the offer, he was afraid of becoming so embroiled in the daily problems and intrigues of an opera house, as he had been during his time with Mamontov, that he would have no time for composing. On the other hand, he liked conducting and had long been seriously attracted to composing operas, so he finally signed a contract for five months. He stayed for two years.

Rakhmaninov's reputation as an uncompromising, strict director preceded him from the Mamontov Opera. This was confirmed in the first rehearsals at the Bolshoi, when he implemented a reform which made history. The conductor had always stood next

'We can say that Rakhmaninov's arrival as the conductor of the Bolshoi Theatre Orchestra immediately breathed new life into it.'

to the prompt box, so as to communicate more easily with the singers, which had meant spending most of his time with his back to the orchestra. Though the singers protested at first, Rakhmaninov had his desk moved onto the podium between the stalls and the orchestra pit, as was customary in other theatres, so that he could exert equal control over both stage and orchestra. In addition he forbade the musicians, especially the brass, to slip out of the pit when they had long periods of rest. Slack, uncoordinated music-making at the Bolshoi was over.[39]

His debut at the beginning of September 1904 with Dargomizhsky's *Rusalka* was a huge success. The influential Moscow critic Nikolay Kashkin summed it up: 'We can say that Rakhmaninov's arrival as conductor of the Bolshoi Theatre orchestra immediately breathed new life into it – something which we dared only dream of in these pages and which is, in our opinion, close to being achieved. I am not talking so much about the artistic rationale of the new conductor as an accompanist as about a new source of musical beauty. This can only be beneficial in provoking a good response from the performers' voices, which are much improved by it. We shall of course follow Mr Rakhmaninov's progress in the profession of opera conductor with the utmost interest, for his work holds a lot of promise for our [musical] scene.'[40]

His other well-received new productions at the Bolshoi included Glinka's *A Life for the Tsar*, Borodin's *Prince Igor*, Mussorgsky's *Boris Godunov* and Tchaikovsky's *Queen of Spades* and *Eugene Onegin*.

In September 1905 Rakhmaninov prepared the Moscow performance of Rimsky-Korsakov's *Pan the Governor* and the composer himself attended the final rehearsals. He and Rakhmaninov had known each other for years, but only now while working together did the conductor appreciate what a sensitive musician the composer was, gifted with a finely tuned ear and a highly developed sense for musical colour. Rimsky-Korsakov, for his part, was impressed with the thorough musical preparation and confident manner of his young colleague. The two of them discovered an affinity which transcended the old rivalries between the Moscow and St Petersburg schools. Rakhmaninov's interest in Rimsky-Korsakov's works now began to deepen and during the next years he studied his great operas in detail. In exile in America he once said in passing that Rimsky was possibly the greatest Russian composer.[41]

The success of Rakhmaninov's work at the Bolshoi begs the question: what prevented him from pursuing a career as a conductor? The conditions were favourable enough, as the Bolshoi was flourishing, which helped to increase his existing reputation even more and led to invitations to conduct symphony concerts. However, his primary vocation was as a composer, and conducting and performing as a pianist meant nothing more to him than ways of earning money.

The relatively scanty accounts of Rakhmaninov the conductor all concur that he was one of the few who could produce an absolutely personal sound from the orchestra, just as his astonishing talent as a pianist could place the 'Rakhmaninov stamp' on any piece from any period. It is worth quoting an interesting observation from Alexander Goldenweiser, according to whom the conductor surpassed the pianist in the rigour of his interpretation: '. . . Rakhmaninov the conductor was, in terms of rhythm, considerably stricter and more restrained. His performance as a conductor was distinguished by the same force of temperament and had the same impact upon the audience, but it was considerably stricter and truer than his performance as Rakhmaninov the pianist. Where Arthur Nikisch's conducting was beautiful and theatrical, Rakhmaninov's movements were sparing, I might even say primitive, as though he were simply counting out the bars. Still, despite this, his power over both orchestra and audience was utterly irresistible.'[42]

Rakhmaninov was extremely exacting, insistent and even imperious to those he conducted. At rehearsals he would make a lot of comments and was very demanding. His perfect pitch, which was amazingly accurate and unusually keen, and his 'good ear' were very useful to him when rehearsing. Rakhmaninov could actually hear in minute detail the whole of the score being performed. He noticed and corrected not only the musicians' normal errors, but also the tiniest of mistakes, 'imperceptible' inaccuracies that, however loudly the massed orchestra thundered, he consistently strove to put right . . . He didn't ask, but commanded . . . in such a stern tone of voice, that the orchestra had no choice but to fulfil the conductor's orders unquestioningly.

Mikhail Bagrinovsky, *Memoirs,* from *Recollections* vol 2, pp 39/40

Later on, in America, Rakhmaninov only conducted on exceptional occasions, so one can hardly make a relative judgment about his importance and ability as a conductor. Without going as far as Nikolay Medtner, who considered him 'the greatest

Russian conductor',[43] we can at least accept that if he had wanted to he could have competed not only with the most famous Russian conductors of his day (Vassily Safonov and Sergey Koussevitsky) but with the international elite as well. His recordings with the Philadelphia Orchestra confirm the impression of 'rigour' mentioned above – a rigour which always produced great elegance and musicality. But perhaps even these recordings are only limited in their general application, because when he was conducting his own works (*The Isle of the Dead* or the Third Symphony) we can only draw conclusions about how he as composer understood them (or wanted them to be understood), rather than about his particular qualities as conductor.

An interview Rakhmaninov gave in the thirties, in which he spoke of the need for self-discipline as the most important virtue in a conductor, sheds light on him not only in that role but as a pianist and composer as well: *Of all musical gifts, conducting is in a class apart – a personal talent which cannot be acquired. To be a good conductor a musician must possess powers of restraint. He must have the strength to be quiet. And by 'quiet' I do not mean placid and unmoved. The full intensity of musical emotion must be there, but at the heart of it is the quietness of perfect mental poise and controlled power.* He concluded with a remarkable analogy, drawn from the enthusiasm for driving he had already felt when he was living in Russia: *When I conduct, I experience much of the same feeling as when I drive my car – an inner calm that gives me complete mastery of myself and of the forces, musical or mechanical, at my command.*[44]

When he was working at the Mamontov Opera, Rakhmaninov was already seriously interested in composing for the stage. Between 1900 and 1905 he wrote his two one-act operas, *The Miserly Knight* and *Francesca da Rimini*, both of which were premiered at the Bolshoi under his direction. The reception was lukewarm. The critic Yuly Engel remarked that *The Miserly Knight* was not suited to a large stage, but was 'rather a pièce de résistance for his fans, who are able to appreciate the composer's fine filigree writing'.[45] In spite of some remarkable musical detail, neither opera is in fact theatrically effective, mainly due to the choice of text. Pushkin's little tragedy *The Miserly Knight* does not contain enough dialogue and is too weighed down with ideas to be suitable for the stage. *Francesca* is much the same; it does not contain a single dramatically motivated event but consists of a series of single, unrelated scenes. Understandably, to this day neither opera has found a place even in the Russian repertory. He planned two further operas – on Flaubert's *Salammbô* and Maeterlinck's *Monna Vanna* – but they did not get beyond initial plans in one case and rough sketches in the other.

The 1905 Revolution only affected Rakhmaninov remotely. According to Russian sources, he did put his signature to a number of resolutions demanding the establishment of citizens' basic rights, but it is not known if he was any further involved. Even in later years he never explained his attitude to these events; it seems most likely that in those unsettled times he was primarily concerned that political upheavals should affect his opera work as little as possible.

Neither the burden of daily opera-house life nor the lack of success of his own operas led Rakhmaninov to give up his work at the Bolshoi, but rather the overwhelming desire to return to composing in peace. In order to be disturbed as little as possible he decided to spend the winter months in Dresden. The significance of this decision to leave Russia for a prolonged period can be measured against the haste with which he had longed to return home from his previous foreign trips. He had given concerts in England, Poland and Austria and visited Germany, Switzerland and Italy, so why did he choose Dresden? It seems he was fascinated by Germany, its culture and its musical life and in the summer of 1899 he had resumed his study of the German language.[46] After the turmoil of 1905, he also appreciated the

The Old Market Place, Dresden, c 1905 Rakhmaninov was fascinated by Germany; its culture and its musical life.

apparent political stability. According to Natalya, 'during those years he was attracted to the orderliness which then reigned in Germany.'[47] Dresden offered the isolation he desired but also the possibility of taking part in a rich cultural life. The famous Semper Opera was enjoying enormous success under its conductor Ernst Edler von Schuch and the premieres of Richard Strauss's operas were attracting attention way beyond the city.

Having rented a house on the outskirts of Dresden, Rakhmaninov wrote to Russian friends: *We are living here as genuine hermits, seeing nobody, knowing nobody and never showing our faces anywhere. I am working a great deal and feel very well.*[48] In his very first days there he went to the opera: *I heard Strauss's* Salome *here and went into absolute rapture, most of all because of the orchestra, but there was much I liked in the music itself, whenever it didn't sound too insincere. And all the same, Strauss is highly talented and his instrumentation is remarkable. If I, sitting in the theatre and having listened to the whole of* Salome, *had imagined that right there and then they had*

played my opera, I would have felt somehow uncomfortable and embar-
rassed. Exactly as though I had gone out in public naked. Strauss already
knows very well how to dress himself.[49] He also went to Leipzig to hear
the Gewandhaus Orchestra playing under Arthur Nikisch. *Not*
long ago I was in Leipzig for the second time. In the morning I attended
Nikisch's conducting class at the Conservatory. It was very boring, though
the class itself interested me very much. I watched three students of con-
ducting. Poor Nikisch! . . . One of them, an idiot and an impudent
fellow, had the nerve to contradict Nikisch when he said that at this point
he had to beat in six (Tchaikovsky's Fifth Symphony, by the way) and
started demonstrating that it would actually end up being in two. So there
and then he conducted it in two but of course the idiot couldn't bring it off
. . . To crown it all there was the Gewandhaus concert in the evening.
Nikisch was quite exceptionally spirited and also in control. The pro-
gramme only consisted of two symphonies and no soloists – Brahms's First
and Tchaikovsky's Sixth . . . It was brilliant in the truest sense of the
word; it is impossible to surpass that.[50]

In his seclusion in Dresden Rakhmaninov produced three of his
most important works: the Second Symphony op 27, the First
Piano Sonata op 28 and the Symphonic Poem *The Isle of the Dead*
op 29. Presumably with the failure of the First Symphony in
mind, he followed a completely different method in his thematic
structure of the Second. While in the First Symphony he followed
Liszt's technique of metamorphosis (drawing a series of images
from one main theme), in the Second Symphony the themes are
relatively detached, in spite of their latent reference to the 'motto'
of the opening. Not until the finale do they join together and even
then only tenuously. In this sense the Second Symphony is more
conservative and traditional and less experimental or innovative,
but in general definitely richer in invention and content; it is
wonderful to hear broad, flowing melodies springing naturally
out of tiny beginnings. The melodic lines interweave effortlessly;
the resulting counterpoint never sounds academic. The dedication

to Sergey Taneyev is hardly a coincidence; it is a late gesture of recognition to the great Russian master of contrapuntal technique. Many critics have accused this symphony of being diffuse and long-winded, but Rakhmaninov's lyricism needs breadth if it is to flow organically and freely. It is the air of spontaneity and naturalness which make the music so irresistible and compelling, even to the casual listener. In comparison with the First Symphony, the instrumentation is more varied and skilful; as always, the composer favours dark, muted tone colours; the strings underpin the whole structure and the critic Yuly Engel was justified in saying that it was almost like a string symphony.[51]

The first movement (*largo. allegro moderato*) begins with a profound slow introduction. Its opening bars become a 'motto', taken up in every movement, either almost literally or in a modified form, which is also an integral part of the thematic structure of each individual movement. This movement is in sonata form with two ideas – an elegiac main theme in the violins and a pastoral secondary theme introduced by a solo clarinet – but they are not emphatically contrasted and the overriding impression is of one sweeping, lyrical, all-embracing statement. The development section concentrates on the first theme, from which stems a series of strongly emotional climaxes. The fascination of the scherzo which follows in a free rondo form (*allegro motto*) lies in the sharp contrasts in its thematic development, instrumentation and technical structure, and the string fugato in the middle strikes one as extravagant – a foretaste of the later Rakhmaninov and his capacity for irony. The slow movement (*adagio*) is characterised by a grand melodic line out of which multifarious elaboration of the subsidiary parts and intertwining polyphony are drawn and here – quite rarely in a Rakhmaninov slow movement – the prevailing colours are bright and optimistic. As in other contemporary symphonies, the most problematic movement is the finale (*allegro moderato*). Here the composer does in fact succeed in picking up and incorporating thematic material from the previous movements, but the synthesis he aims for is superficial and suffers from the main ideas not being sufficiently varied when they recur.

While the symphonic tradition of the Viennese classical composers and their successors forms the model for the Second Symphony, Liszt's symphonic poetry lies at the root of *The Isle of the Dead*. The work was inspired by an eponymous painting by Arnold Böcklin which Rakhmaninov had only seen in a black-and-white reproduction. Once he had seen the original, he wrote: *I was not much moved by the colour of the painting. If I had seen the original first, I might not have composed my* Isle of the Dead. *I like the picture best in black and white.*[52] The mood is appropriately gloomy and despairing. It opens with an ostinato motif in the bass, joined by short melodic phrases which gradually permeate the whole piece and lead up to the climax. The middle section rejects this mood and Rakhmaninov said about it: *It has to make a powerful contrast to all the rest; it should be played faster, with more excitement and more passion. As this passage does not refer to the picture it is in a way complementary and therefore the contrast is absolutely essential. First*

The Isle of the Dead. Painting by Arnold Böcklin, 1883. National Gallery, Berlin

death, then life.[53] However, the initial mood returns uncompromis-
ingly, announced by a passage of harsh chords. At the close the
'rowing' ostinato rhythm prevails and the pessimistic attitude –
the insight into the inevitability of death – wins the day. The
stereotype phrases and grey hues of *The Isle of the Dead* are deliberately calculated means of expression and the work owes to them
its great inner tension and evocative effect. This is one of
Rakhmaninov's most convincing symphonic works in which
dimension and content are happily blended.

The same spirit permeates both the First Piano Sonata and the
Second Symphony. Though tending to be monumental, they
belong to the classical tradition and hint at their creator's desire
and claim to be accepted as a 'great' composer. The First Piano
Sonata is perhaps Rakhmaninov's most all-embracing and mean-
ingful piano work, and while composing it he wrote to his close
friend Nikita Morosov: *The sonata is irrepressibly wild and endlessly
long – I think about 45 minutes. I was drawn to the project by such
dimensions or, more precisely, by one overriding idea. It is of three contrasting figures from a work of world literature. Of course there will be
no mention of this in the programme, though it crossed my mind that if I
made it clear what my aim was the sonata would become a little easier to
understand. No-one is ever going to play this composition because it is too
long and too difficult but, perhaps most importantly, because of its dubi-
ous musical value. At one point I wanted to turn it into a symphony, but
that proved impossible because of the pure pianistic style in which it is
written.*[54]

Rakhmaninov later gave some details of the Sonata's programme to the pianist Konstantin Igumnov, who was to give the
premiere: 'I heard from him [Rakhmaninov] that he had Goethe's
Faust in mind when he was composing it: the first movement represented Faust, the second Marguerite and the third the flight to
the Brocken and Mephistopheles.'[55] Nevertheless, the First Sonata
should not be regarded as programme music in the narrower

sense, for the programme primarily serves the composer's conception during the creative process. It is only of secondary importance for a musical listener's deeper comprehension. A leitmotif links all three movements, based on the interval of a perfect fifth. As with the Second Symphony, the final movement is conceived as a synthesis, with motifs from the previous movements repeatedly recurring. On the whole, however, it is as unsatisfactory as the finale of the Symphony, because the composer's attempt to make the last movement the centre of gravity once again leads to a certain long-windedness. The many unnecessary repetitions hinder the essential dramatic urgency. The piano writing is extremely complicated and tends to be overcharged. To this day it has led a shadowy existence – admittedly more on account of its extreme technical demands than of its musical qualities.

I am now working hard but I would like to do a lot more in the last month left to me before returning to Moscow. My opinion of the new works is always the same: they are difficult for me to write and I am discontented with myself. It is a permanent anguish.

Rakhmaninov to Nikita Morosov,
21 March 1909

Even in Dresden, Rakhmaninov did not find composing easy and as before he went through phases of being plagued by self-doubt about his work. He was not able to dedicate himself exclusively to composition, because for financial reasons he had to accept offers of concerts and, besides, he hoped to promote and publicise his works by conducting and playing them. In the spring of 1907 he performed in the series of Russian Concerts in Paris organised by the impresario Sergey Diaghilev. This was a genuine invitation, while it showed that he now belonged to the elite circle of Russian composers – among them Rimsky-Korsakov, Glazunov and Scriabin – who were acclaimed as the representatives of contemporary Russian music. In early 1908 he conducted his Second Symphony in St Petersburg and Moscow and was also giving performances – mostly as soloist in his Second

Natalya and Sergey Rakhmaninov in Dresden, 1907

Concerto but occasionally also as conductor or in a chamber ensemble – in Warsaw, Berlin, London, Frankfurt and various towns in Holland. He was also officially honoured as a composer:

the Belyayev Foundation (founded by the St Petersburg publisher Mitrofan Belyayev) awarded him the Glinka Prize several times – in 1904 for his Second Piano Concerto, in 1906 for the Cantata *Spring* and in 1908 for his Second Symphony.

While engaged at the Bolshoi Theatre, Rakhmaninov had also been conducting symphony concerts since 1904. Two music enthusiasts, a Monsieur and Madame Kersin, had founded the Society of Lovers of Russian Music and mounted the so-called Kersin Concerts, for which they engaged him as conductor. From then on he was well known to the Moscow public as a conductor of Russian orchestral music. In the spring of 1909 Arthur Nikisch cancelled a series of symphonic concerts for the Russian Music Society and the authorities quickly asked Rakhmaninov to take his place. As a result of gentle pressure from several Muscovite musicians and music-lovers who wanted to involve him more closely in Russian musical life, he was also made Vice-President of the Russian Music Society.

His return to Moscow was fixed for the spring of 1909. Before setting off, he wrote to Sergey Taneyev: *How pleasant it is here in Dresden, Sergey Ivanovich! If you only knew how sad I am that this is to be the last winter I spend here! If you ask me why I am not staying any longer, I shall reply that, first of all, the Music Society's affairs and concerts are calling me to Moscow and that secondly, I also have a contract in relation to Dresden – this time not with an agent but with my wife, the upshot of which is that I promised we would not spend more than three years abroad. And that time has already passed . . .*[56]

At the Zenith (1909–1917)

As usual, Rakhmaninov spent the summer of 1909 at Ivanovka, where he was preparing for a late autumn tour of America. In the space of only a few weeks he composed his Third Piano Concerto for this tour – a work which has in recent decades become nearly as popular as the Second Concerto, not only due to its musical charm but also to its exorbitant technical difficulties. There are few works which demand from the player such strength and stamina together with artistry and elegance. Even Rakhmaninov, whose technique was ideally suited to his compositions, had to practise it intensively on the crossing to America.

The concerto is dedicated to the Polish pianist Josef Hofmann the only pianist whom Rakhmaninov (not entirely without modesty) considered his equal. In fact Hofmann never played it, and

Polish pianist Josef Hofmann (1876–1957) was one of the world's genuine child prodigies of genius. Hofmann became the sole private pupil of Anton Rubinstein in Berlin, who declared emphatically that he did not believe in child prodigies – except for Hofmann! In addition to Hofmann's illustrious performing and recording career, he became the Director of the famed Curtis Institute in Philadelphia from 1927 to 1938. Rakhmaninov dedicated his Third Piano Concerto to Hofmann, who curiously never performed the work.

When Rakhmaninov was asked who he considered to be the most important pianists of the age, he replied, *Hofmann . . . and myself!* The mutual admiration these pianists had for each other was enormous and deeply heartfelt. After hearing Hofmann play his Second Piano Concerto, Rakhmaninov felt he revealed inner beauties that he had not known to exist.

apart from the composer its first noted interpreters were Vladimir Horovitz and Walter Gieseking. Rakhmaninov even said later that Horovitz played it better than he did. Since then the Third Concerto has been played by numerous younger pianists and is very popular at major piano competitions, such as the Tchaikovsky Competition in Moscow, though it runs the risk of being reduced to a mere technical tour de force.

The opening of the first movement (*allegro ma non tanto*) is, like its two predecessors, very characteristic of the composer. The piano presents a simple, folk-like melody while the orchestra stays

No other pianist was more closely associated with Rakhmaninov than Vladimir Horovitz. Rakhmaninov became a mentor and invaluable father figure to the younger Horovitz. Rakhmaninov first heard of him after receiving an enthusiastic letter from Kreisler, describing the enormous success this young pianist was having performing the Third Piano Concerto in Europe. This immediately aroused Rakhmaninov's curiosity since he had never enjoyed much popular success with that work. Upon Horovitz's arrival in New York for his Carnegie Hall debut, he was invited by Rakhmaninov to meet him in the now legendary Steinway basement for a play-through of the Third Concerto. For Horovitz, this was to be his true American debut – a chance to meet and play for his childhood hero and musical god. Horovitz was terribly nervous at this encounter, with Rakhmaninov accompanying him on a second piano. After the meeting, Rakhmaninov remarked to a friend that Horovitz *swallowed the concerto whole!*

in the background. The simplicity and charm of the theme might lead the listener to assume that it came from Russian folk or church music, but Rakhmaninov insisted: *The first theme of my Third Concerto is derived neither from the form of the folk song nor from church sources. It simply wrote itself! . . . If I had a plan when composing this theme, it was just how it should sound. I wanted to 'sing' a tune on the piano like a singer does and find an appropriate orchestral accompaniment, that is, one which would not drown this 'song'. That's all! . . . Just the same, I find that, against my will, this theme does take on a song-like or familiar quality.*[57]

In contrast to the epic, narrative nature of the main theme, which swiftly intensifies and erupts in a brief cadenza, the secondary theme is dreamy and lyrical and evolves into a dialogue between soloist and orchestra before alternating between drama and cheerful playfulness. The development section takes up the first theme, gives it new tone colours and draws it up into a powerful climax. At the end the soloist plays a grandiose and highly virtuoso cadenza which logically embodies the dynamic climax of the movement. Of the composer's two versions of the cadenza, the first is shorter and easier to play than the second. Vladimir Horovitz remarked: 'I play the original one. Rakhmaninov always played it, too . . . That cadenza really builds to the end of the movement. The alternate cadenza is like an ending in itself. It's not good to end the concerto before it's over! . . . Rakhmaninov was a tremendous virtuoso. What he wrote was wonderful and he could play it. But later, when he looked at it musically in relation to his whole concerto, he knew it wasn't right. He didn't play it. So I don't.'[58] As an interesting formal innovation, the cadenza replaces the recapitulation and so the coda can confine itself to a brief reprise of the two main themes.

The wistful orchestral introduction to the second movement (*intermezzo. adagio*) is the starting point for a set of sonorous variations, led by the piano from the outset. The initial lyricism gradually darkens. The last variation is surprisingly a waltz, as elegantly transparent as it is sparklingly virtuoso. The finale follows on without a break. Its main theme is rhythmically elastic and its secondary theme a triumphant march; both are pianistically extremely elegant and display great strength. The spacious climaxes contain repeats of the lyrical and scherzo-style episodes without ever prejudicing their grand dramatic line. A solemn hymn brings the work to an end in a brilliant major key.

Rakhmaninov correcting the 3rd concerto at Ivanovko

The Third Piano Concerto marks the culmination of the Romantic piano concerto; its level of technical virtuosity long seemed unsurpassable. In contrast to the Second Concerto, in the Third the piano part asserts itself much more strongly against the orchestra; the soloist is always dominant and seeks to dictate to the orchestra, which is, however, significantly more than mere accompaniment, as it is in many 19th-century virtuoso concertos. It partners the piano as a potential equal while not overwhelming it, while the piano challenges the orchestra by means of masterful polyphony and the use of every available register. This contrast gives the Third Piano Concerto an irresistible charm and richness.

Rakhmaninov's observations about the folk music element in the themes of this concerto could be applied to all his compositions. Conscious or even attributable borrowings from folk music are exceptions (for instance, in the Piano Pieces for Four Hands

Rakhmaninov portrait by Robert Sterl, April 1909

op 11 and in the Three Russian Songs op 41). Though much of his music sounds Russian, and evokes associations with folk music, these are just involuntarily subjective impulses, either in mood or in melodic and rhythmical language. What at first sounds like folk music is on closer examination always attributable to the composer's creative individuality. Rakhmaninov had no feeling for overt musical nationalism. Even though he was interested in Russian folk song and even more so in the Orthodox liturgy, he did not consider quoting them literally in his compositions. The 'Western' influence in his musical training may well have had a significant effect on his relationship with the Russian element in music, leading him to believe that it was undesirable to instil anything specifically Russian into his works. He felt himself to be a Russian, steeped in Russian traditions, so his music could not be anything else.

To what extent and in what sense the term 'folk music' should be used is debatable, but if one accepts that any music can *become* in some way folk music, at least some of Rakhmaninov's works can be counted as such. Every Russian knows the Second Piano Concerto and associates it with the Minute's Silence on Victory Day, observed in remembrance of the sacrifices of the Great Patriotic War (1941–1945), after which it is traditionally played. The *Vocalise* op 34, no 14 is equally well known, also recalling those sacrifices. One might be inclined to reject such functional-ising of Rakhmaninov's music but that cannot alter the fact that millions of Russians identify with it, regarding it as the most Russian of all Russian music.

Rakhmaninov's American tour in 1909/10 was a great success. The American press gave the Third Concerto a cool reception at its world premiere in New York (under Walter Damrosch), but the public liked it. Just as on his visit to England in 1899, he was hailed as the genius who had just composed the C-sharp minor Prelude, which had been widely performed without bringing him any financial reward (it was not under copyright!). Although he had meanwhile suffered from the popularity of this composition, he realised that he owed his invitation to America to it. He said to one American journalist: *Under the circumstances I should be thankful, I suppose, that I wrote the composition. But I am undecided whether my oversight in neglecting to secure international copyright for it was altogether fortunate for me. Had I copyrighted it, I might have had wealth as well as fame from it . . . I took the precaution to have {the ten Preludes of op 23} copyrighted by a German publisher. I think them far better music than my first Prelude, but the public has shown no disposi-tion to share my belief. I cannot tell whether my judgment is at fault or whether the existence of that copyright has been a blight on their popular-ity. Consequently it will always be an open question with me whether intrinsic merit or absence of copyright is responsible for the success of my earlier work.*[59]

The Third Concerto was performed again in New York in January 1910 under Gustav Mahler. Working with him was a rev-elation for Rakhmaninov. *At that time Mahler was the only conductor whom I considered worthy to be classed with Nikisch. He touched my com-poser's heart straight away by devoting himself to my Concerto until the accompaniment, which is rather complicated, had been practised to the point of perfection, although he had already gone through another long rehearsal. According to Mahler, every detail of the score was important –*

an attitude which is unfortunately rare among conductors.[60]

Rakhmaninov undertook the American tour more for financial reasons (the agreed fees were high for him – 1000 roubles a concert), than out of any inner compulsion or curiosity, and the incessant travelling and the stressful succession of performances put a great strain on him. His general impression of America was not favourable; he wrote to one of his relations that the country was cold and its people only cared for business. He did not like the American public either and told a Moscow newspaper on his return: *The public is amazingly cold and spoilt by touring companies with first-class artists. They are always looking for something extraordinary, different to the rest. The local newspapers dutifully record how many times you were called for an encore and for the general public this seems to be the measure of your talent.*[61]

By 1910 at the latest Rakhmaninov was one of the most important figures both in Moscow musical life and Russian music in general. He was Vice-President of the Russian Music Society, Permanent Conductor of the Moscow Philharmonic Society and Artistic Consultant to the Russian Music Publishing Company, founded by Sergey Koussevitzky in 1909. However, conflicts within the Russian musical establishment were beginning to intensify. Alexander Scriabin and his disciples were enriching the major-minor keys with more and more new and additional notes and around 1910 abandoned them altogether. Scriabin (and even more his followers) asserted that theirs was the only correct and consistent musical path, and they fell out with traditionally-minded musicians. The musical press was soon writing of two irreconcilable groups: the 'moderns' around Scriabin and the conservatives around Rakhmaninov. Partisans on both sides incessantly provoked each other without either composer being involved. When Rakhmaninov played his Third Concerto in Moscow in the spring of 1910, he had to endure the composer and critic Grigory Kreyn saying that it contained nothing 'but feeble themes with monotonous, meandering solo passages, resting on an unoriginal harmony'.[62]

Though some individual members of the Moscow press were openly hostile to Rakhmaninov, they ultimately stood by him out of a sort of local pride. 'It would be wholly unjust to deny Rakhmaninov's enormous talent, as several St Petersburg critics mainly do,'[63] wrote Leonid Sabaneyev, Scriabin's close friend in Moscow. One of his worst detractors was the St Petersburg critic Viacheslav Karatygin, an ardent champion of modernism who missed no opportunity to needle him. After the Revolution, when entirely new musical battle-lines had been drawn up, Karatygin remained faithful to his anti-Rakhmaninov attitude. In a 1923 review of the 19-year old Vladimir Horovitz playing the First Piano Concerto in Leningrad, he wrote: 'I do not like Rakhmaninov. What few fragments of music there are in the concerto played by Horovitz in which harmony or melody are sufficiently balanced sink without trace into the general grey, noisy mass, producing an impression of a deluge in a desert.' Horovitz admittedly came to the rescue of the concerto: 'However, where a performance of the piano part reaches such heights as it does in Horovitz's execution, even Rakhmaninov's music compels one to listen and even to experience some sort of push and pull of psychic energy, by virtue of its proximity to the dynamics of aesthetic emotion.'[64]

The relationship between Rakhmaninov and Scriabin was proof against the sniping of their followers. They had known each other since childhood, had both 'enjoyed' Zverev's schooling and studied under Arensky and Taneyev at the Moscow Conservatory. Crucially, their composing had similar origins: both were outstanding pianists and they revered Liszt and Chopin, whose works they emulated in very different ways. Rakhmaninov did not like Scriabin's harmonic innovations, which heralded an end to the world of late-Romantic music, nor his theosophical mysticism

Alexander Scriabin

and pseudo-religious ideas on redemption. Such hocus-pocus was fundamentally alien to him. As their musical viewpoints diverged, so did their lives. Though they had never been friends, they were good old acquaintances. However, they were competitors and each was afraid of being overshadowed by the other's success.

Natalya reports on an occurrence which throws light on this rivalry. When Scriabin played his own Piano Concerto in F-sharp minor op 20 in December 1911 under Rakhmaninov's baton, he thought he should test the latter's ability as a conductor and for once really make him sweat, as he explained to the orchestra. Irritated because the rehearsal had passed without incident, Scriabin got drunk before the concert. 'Scriabin in his agitation forgot himself when he was playing, leaving out passages and passing over bars. Sergey Vassilievich kept having to catch up with him but they finished together all the same. Never again did Sergey Vassilievich suffer such agonies as he had to for this performance by Scriabin.'[65]

In return, Rakhmaninov was tempted to be tactless about Scriabin's 'modern' music. Alexander Osovsky, sometime member of the artistic council of the Russian Music Publishing House, remembers the following event. During a publishers' meeting attended by Scriabin, Rakhmaninov caught sight of the score of his *Prometheus*, which he had never seen. (This was a late orchestral composition into which Scriabin introduced a 'colour piano' to 'paint the background' for the music with light effects.) Rakhmaninov took the score and sat down at the piano. 'The famous first chord of *Prometheus* amazed and even enraptured him but further on pointed remarks followed one after the other, then a perplexed shrugging of the shoulders and smiles. "What colour is this music?" he asked ironically about the *tastiera per luce*. "It isn't music, Sergey Vassilievich, but atmosphere enveloping the audience – a violet atmosphere," replied Scriabin. "This chord won't work, the orchestral parts are arranged illogically," was the next remark Rakhmaninov threw at him. "But I need it to sound exactly like that," retorted Scriabin. Rakhmaninov mercilessly continued to pour buckets of cold water over the composer's head. Scriabin could not stand it, angrily slammed down the score, stopped playing and invited anyone who wanted to come to his house that evening to hear the *Poem of Fire,* which he himself would play with the colour piano, especially adapted in his studio.'[66]

Around 1910 there was talk about a third Moscow composer, Nikolay Medtner (1880–1951), in addition to Rakhmaninov and Scriabin. Medtner came from a Baltic German family.[67] Also both pianist and composer, he wrote principally for the keyboard, though he also composed a large number of songs and chamber music. Like Rakhmaninov, he felt firmly rooted in tradition, but less the Russian than the German, as personified by Beethoven and Brahms. Rakhmaninov particularly admired his early works and after hearing his First Piano Sonata op 5 he predicted a brilliant future for him.

Though Rakhmaninov and Medtner were in close contact from 1913 on, their personal relationship was complicated, and clouded by the influence of Medtner's brother Emil, a philosopher

Nikolay Medtner (1880–1951) suffered inexplicable neglect during his lifetime. A significant composer for the piano, Medtner doggedly pursued a more conservative musical style, fusing elements of German and Russian musical heritage into a unique language, contrary to the rising tide of 'modernism.' Medtner's treatise, *The Muse and the Fashion*, set out his philosophy. He felt that the source of all music was the 'mythical first song, the theme and contents of musical creation'. The composer's job was to uncover this heavenly song.

Leaving Russia in 1921, he briefly lived in Paris, but finally settled in London, where his concerts and music were better received. Medtner remained an isolated figure, composing in monastic seclusion but denied the worldwide fame that blessed Rakhmaninov after his exile.

and art expert whose ideas were alien to Rakhmaninov. Marietta Shaginian (1888–1982), a poet and writer friend of the Medtners and a confidante of Rakhmaninov, recalls: 'The conversations at the Medtners' house were always strange. They began with a concrete thesis about art or science . . . and then got buried in all sorts of philosophical discussions and reflections . . . Sergey Vassilievich did not like these conversations at all; he was afraid of them and never joined in. He could not bear abstractions; they embarrassed him in the same way that some people are embarrassed by intimate matters and they even made him blush . . . As the Medtners could not just talk freely and happily 'about nothing' . . . that is, keep up normal dinner-table conversation, which can also be fascinating and is useful in its own way, there was hardly any conversation to be had with him at all.'[68]

At the beginning of 1912 Rakhmaninov received a letter from Marietta Shaginian signed with the pseudonym 'Re'. It was not the usual kind of fan letter but contained her spirited impressions of his music and his performances. Touched by 'Re's' effusive style he replied and their correspondence developed into a personal relationship which lasted until 1917. The poetess sensed intuitively that he was unsettled by the conflicting musical trends and had suffered a creative crisis. To tell the truth, it is astounding to find Rakhmaninov the established composer acknowledging his former sufferings so openly: *I love your letters, because in them, on every line, I find faith, hope and love directed at me. This is the balm with which I heal my spiritual wounds, albeit rather shyly and falteringly, but you describe me amazingly accurately and you know me very well . . . My 'criminal spiritual straitjacket' (from your letter) is unfortunately all too evident and my 'perdition in philistinism' (from the same) seems to me just as it seems to you – located in the not too distant future. It is all true! It is true because I believe in you. Teach me to believe in myself, dear Re, even only half as much as you believe in me. If I have ever believed in myself it was a long time ago, in my youth! . . . This malady nags at me persistently and as the years go by it spreads, alas, ever deeper. It will not be surprising if I decide in a short while to give up composing altogether . . .*[69]

The contact with Marietta Shaginian was as fruitful for Rakhmaninov personally as it was artistically, as he found it peculiarly attractive to talk to the young woman about himself and his music. He asked her to help him choose poems to set to music and about half the texts of the Songs op 34 were her suggestions. Though he had regretted the sombreness of the poems he set in his op 26 and feared they would bring on his depression while he was composing them, the orientation of op 34 was clear-cut: *The mood is more sad than cheerful; bright timbres come ill to me!*[70]

When Rakhmaninov left Russia all contact with Marietta ceased, but less because of that circumstance than because she was a committed Communist. She later wrote an admiring biography of Stalin and her political affiliations probably alienated her from him.

At the end of 1912 Rakhmaninov withdrew from concerts and other commitments in order to relax completely for a while. After brief spells in Germany and Switzerland he spent several months

with his family in Rome and would have stayed there longer had his daughters not been taken ill. Once again he embarked on two major works while living outside Russia, as happened during his time in Dresden – this time *The Bells* op 35 and the Second Piano Sonata op 36. Apparently change of atmosphere and unfamiliar surroundings were needed to stimulate large-scale works.

Rakhmaninov's choral works and operas had a chequered history. While *The Miserly Knight* – and to a

Marietta Shaginian

greater extent *Francesca* – are theatrically problematic, in places resembling oratorios, the operatic baritone aria in the cantata *Spring* evokes a true stage atmosphere. In *The Bells* he created a hybrid of the oratorio and orchestral genres, and called it a 'choral symphony', stressing its symphonic nature.

The Bells is based on a story by Edgar Allan Poe, in a poetic adaptation by Konstantin Balmont. It evokes four different types of tintinnabulation and their symbolism: silvery sleigh-bells for birth and youth, golden bells for wedding, copper for storms and iron for mourning. Rakhmaninov spoke of what lay behind this:

The sound of church bells dominated all the cities of the Russia I used to know – Novgorod, Kiev, Moscow. They accompanied every Russian from childhood to the grave, and no composer could escape their influence . . . All my life I have taken pleasure in the differing moods and music of gladly chiming and mournfully tolling bells . . . With Poe's verses before me, I heard the bell voices and tried to set down on paper their lovely tones that seemed to express the varying shades of human experience.[71]

This is no naturalistic imitation; the sonority of the bells is artfully transmuted into the orchestration, where complex colours of pealing and striking express inner changes of mood. The subject matter of *The Bells* recalls *The Isle of the Dead,* but here life and death clash less, portrayed as complementary elements in the four stages of life. The underlying mood of the work is set by the final movement: the tragedy of death and the despair of mourning.

The forces required – chorus, augmented orchestra and tenor, soprano and baritone soloists – make *The Bells* Rakhmaninov's largest-scale composition. However, his highly refined tone painting opens up a recognisably new sphere of composition. The huge forces are hardly ever used to produce a dense body of sound but are primarily deployed to create a broad tonal palette. The individual movements are linked through the use of leitmotifs and similarities of tone colour and harmony.

The first movement with tenor solo (*Allegro ma non tanto*) portrays youthful enthusiasm and exuberance in strong, bright colours which announce optimism and confidence, over which fleeting shadows are cast by the elegiac middle section and its rocking rhythm. The *Lento* which follows (soprano solo) is the lyrical core of the work but less the description of a wedding, as related in the text, than of melancholy, yearning anticipation, echoing his *Vocalise* op 34. The demonic *Presto* of the third movement plunges us into the negative sphere and the musical setting

Rakhmaninov, an early and passionate automobile enthusiast, at the wheel of his Mercedes-Benz 'Lorelei' in 1912

illustrates the obvious dramatic aspects – 'Noise of the storm', 'Song of the fire' – with an unusual stridency for Rakhmaninov, which makes one forget the 'mental anguish' mentioned in the prologue. The last movement (*lento lugubre*) grows entirely out of the cor anglais's lament, taken up by the baritone solo. This is a farewell finale in late-Romantic vein, echoing not only Tchaikovsky's Sixth Symphony but also Wagner and Mahler.

Reactions to *The Bells* were divided. Some criticised Balmont's problematic poetry for its influence on the composition and particularly on the relatively free type of setting. Several music critics and composers, among them Yuly Engel and Nikolay Myaskovsky, even argued that there was an incongruity between the tenor of the words and the musical forces deployed. The composer may have recognised that his kind of lyricism was incompatible with such material; in any case, he ventured no further along this path. It is hardly a coincidence that when he composed his *Vespers* shortly afterwards, he veered in the opposite direction towards extreme ascetic reserve.

The music derives its essential charm and timbre from the sound of the bells. The underlying idea of conveying these natural sounds or impressions of them permeates all Rakhmaninov's oeuvre. Consider his piano music: 'dancing bells' in the E major Prelude, 'strokes of bells' in the C major Prelude, the 'sounds of little frozen bells' in the A minor Prelude, 'peaceful funeral bells' in the G-sharp minor Prelude – one can go on listing references which especially appeal to Russian listeners, whose traditions endow them with a heightened awareness and appreciation of the pealing of bells.

The Second Sonata in B-flat minor op 36 was written very soon after *The Bells*. In contrast to the academic character of the First Sonata it is varied, strongly inspired and more interestingly written for the pianist, which makes it much more popular with performers. Its weakness is a tendency towards pomposity and a certain ponderousness. Rakhmaninov was unhappy with this work for other reasons: . . . *in this sonata so many voices are moving simultaneously, and it is too long. Chopin's Sonata lasts nineteen minutes, and all has been said.*[72] Vladimir Horovitz, its most sympathetic interpreter, thought Rakhmaninov's 1931 revision too drastically abridged and, with Rakhmaninov's approval, made his own version, a combination of the original and the revised versions.

The centre of gravity of Rakhmaninov's piano music remains in the smaller works, not because he lacked the vision for larger-scale works, but more because he seemed to like restricting himself to brief, sketchy ideas. His critical attitude to his larger works points indirectly to this: he thought them too long and their ideas too diffused. Later in life when living abroad he reflected on this problem: *Young composers are often apt to look condescendingly upon the smaller forms of music . . . A small piece can become as lasting a masterpiece as a large work. As a matter of fact, I have often found that a short piece for the piano has always given me much more pain, and has presented to me many more problems, than a symphony or a concerto. Somehow, in writing for the orchestra, the variety of colours provided by the instruments brings me many different ideas and effects. But when I write a small piece for the piano, I am at the mercy of my thematic idea, which must be presented concisely and without digression.*[73]

Rakhmaninov and his daughter Irina at Ivanovko 1913

The two sets of Études-Tableaux Op 33 and Op 39, written in 1911 and 1916/17 respectively, are masterpieces of concision. The unprecedented title indicates a synthesis of concert studies and tone poems. He does not actually address any particular technical problems and poetic inspiration completely dominates the opulent, virtuoso writing which enhances every detail of these 'study' pieces. The Études resemble the Preludes both in size and content and might seem to be their successors, but from the very first bars they surpass the earlier works in their evocative tone painting. Though their title points to the pictorial, the individual pieces have no specific content. A poetic idea was always just the spur for Rakhmaninov's creativity and never the objective of the music itself.

When in 1930 the Italian composer Ottorino Respighi suggested orchestrating some of the Études, Rakhmaninov gave him the following explanations: op 39, no 2 portrayed sea and seagulls, op 39, no 6 figures from *Little Red Riding Hood*, op 33, no 7 a fair-ground and op 39, no 9 an oriental march. About op 39, no 7 (a funeral march), he said: *The initial theme is a march. The other theme represents the singing of a choir. Commencing with the movement in 16ths in C minor and a little further on in E-flat minor a fine rain is suggested, incessant and hopeless. This movement develops, culminating in C minor – the chimes of a church. The Finale returns to the first theme, a march.*[74] However definite these explanations sound, they are not binding. Though they do testify to the composer's programmatic ideas for his music, they were a private matter for him and not intended for publication. He was not a composer of programme music, in the literal sense of the term. Some of his works are based on programmes, such as *The Isle of the Dead*, but in general any poetic concept remains firmly in the background. This faith in the primary musical qualities of composition testifies to his roots in the classical tradition; he only occasionally ventured into Liszt's territory of explicit musical narrative.

While still at the Conservatory, Rakhmaninov was much taken with old Russian church music and became very interested in attempts to revive it artistically. Though not a believer, awareness of Russian tradition gave him a feeling for the liturgy and he was much attracted to the exclusively vocal music of the Orthodox Church (which is in turn related to traditional Russian folk song) as an expression of his country's ancient past. He adopted this tone of expression, without any historical objective, in his two great works for four-part chorus a cappella – the *Liturgy of St John Chrysostom* op 31 (1910) and the *Vespers* op 37 (1915). The latter particularly shows how thoroughly he understood old Russian church music and its performance as well as with what delicacy, he could use it in a composition.

In the 18th century the Russian monophonic chants were replaced with polyphonic choral hymns, in imitation of Western European fashion. As a result, even in cases where an old liturgical tune was retained as the leading part, the generally accepted type of church music was Western (Italianised), in expression and character and no longer felt specifically Russian. In the train of awakening national consciousness in the 19th century, efforts were made towards a fundamental renovation of church music, and two trends emerged: one, represented by Russian Orthodox circles, insisted on the music's deep-rooted liturgical function and set narrow restrictions on any attempt to develop it artistically; the other, backed by musicians, demanded artistic freedom in the hope that the liturgy would modernise. The Orthodox Church authorities rejected even cautious artistic development in the form of a cappella choral music and not only forbade the performance of the 'new' church music during services but fought against liturgical texts being sung outside the church. It did temporarily succeed in sabotaging the publication of works which it deemed unsuitable, for instance Tchaikovsky's *Liturgy* op 41, but the advance of 'new' church music could hardly be hindered any more. Paradoxically, this process emanated from and was promoted by originally religious institutions such as the Moscow School for Church Music and its associated Synodical Choir, where two outstanding and vigorous personalities – the researchers and musicians Alexander Kastalsky and Stephan Smolensky (to whom the *Vespers* were dedicated) – were active at the beginning of the 20th century.

While Tchaikovsky's 1878 *Liturgy* and 1881 *Vespers* stand at the beginning of this progress, Rakhmaninov's two works with the same names represent its culmination – the end of a historical process which was abruptly broken off by the October Revolution. This applies not least to the relative importance of these works, for while Tchaikovsky's are little more than minor compositions (he himself spoke modestly of polyphonic 'arrangements') Rakhmaninov's, especially the *Vespers*, are key works.

Like the Roman Catholic Church, the Russian Orthodox (Byzantine) Church observes the 'hours' with fixed times for prayer and ritual. On the eve of Sundays and feast days the evening and morning prayers are combined in one rite (the Russian title of the *Vespers* means literally 'watching through the night'), which provides the formula for Rakhmaninov's work, divided into *Vespers* or evening prayers and *Matutin* or morning prayers. The words of the *Vespers*, like those of the *Liturgy*, are based on religious texts, but in ten of the fifteen sections of the former work the composer uses old church chants, whereas all the music of the latter is his own invention. Literal quotations are very rare, however. In most items Rakhmaninov changes the details, by using transposition to improve the development and cuts for greater impact and by varying the harmonies. Where he uses his own tunes, they are indistinguishable from those he quotes. He described it as *stylistic forgery*.[75]

Rakhmaninov's melodies all flow in broad, sweeping motions – an impression underlined by his free and varied metres, as for instance in nos 1 and 3 and in others where the bar lines serve merely as indicators and have no rhythmic function. This free metre is also important for the text, because it allows the rhythm to follow the stress and meaning of every single word. The compositional technique is extraordinarily rich. For example, he sets small sections of the chorus or solo voices against the full choir in the tradition of 17th- and 18th-century Russian part-songs, contrasting tone colours by combining homogeneous and non-homogeneous elements. He divides the main melody polyphonically by modifying the form of variations in the style of Russian folk music and its polyphonic treatment of subsidiary parts. Western-style imitative devices such as fugues and canons are nowhere to be found. In keeping with the simple diatonic nature of the

Rakhmaninov and his daughters Irina and Tatiana at Ivanovko

melodies, Rakhmaninov avoids excessive chromaticism but still creates a synthesis, blending the rich thirds and sixths of the folk music idiom in archaic-sounding phrases and combining Romantic lushness of timbre with austere two-part writing. Tone colour effects and tone painting are extensively used, as in the evocation of the sound of bells – most striking in nos 7 and 12 – the cradle-song in no 5 and the changing light in no 4 (entitled 'gentle light'). A high level of technical skill pervades both the individual pieces and the overall dramatic content and contradicts any impression of slack formal structure. The varied verse and rondo forms follow Russian models, whether from folk music or not. While the first section is primarily lyrical, the second has strongly epic features and its formal layout and composition are notably more complex. The climax of the cycle is the *Great Doxology* (*Great Hymn of Praise*) in no 12, based on an old religious chant of only four notes, from which Rakhmaninov creates a colourfully contrasted tone painting of almost theatrical plasticity. The last three numbers – 13 to 15 – form a finale; their concision resembles chamber music more than a concertante work.

To this day the quality of this work is scarcely recognised, at least not outside Russia. In *Vespers* Rakhmaninov holds in check his typical pliable, passionate and darkly expressive lyricism and frees himself of any tendency towards pathos and religiosity. Thereby the work gains in meditative strength, credibility and expressive objectivity.

The world premiere was given by the Moscow Synodical Choir under Nikolay Danilin on 10 March 1915 as a benefit concert for war victims. The choir's singing contributed to the deep impression it made and five more performances were given, but when all religious music was banned after the Revolution the work disappeared from Russian musical life. Only after *perestroika* was it fittingly acknowledged and appreciated. One problem for modern listeners (aside from the high demands it makes of the choir) is its ambivalent position in musical classification – it is neither suitable nor practical for liturgical use as it lasts over an hour, nor is it a truly secular concert work. As a result it hovers between two worlds; this point is discussed at every performance.

Rakhmaninov himself thought *Vespers* his best composition after *The Bells*. *My favourite passage in this work . . . is the fifth hymn, 'Lord, now lettest Thou Thy servant depart in peace' {Luke ii. 29}. I would like this to be sung at my funeral.*[76]

When the First World War broke out, Russia was cut off from Europe and Rakhmaninov's overseas concerts came to an end. In the previous years he had been a frequent visitor to England, where he had a high reputation and was scheduled to conduct the English premiere of *The Bells* in the autumn of 1914. The war caused an economic crisis in Russian musical life, with publishers and impresarios struggling for survival. As a result Rakhmaninov found himself increasingly performing in Russia and embarking on long tours to remote cities. Though he did so for financial reasons, from the outbreak of the war he devoted part of his earnings to charity.

When Alexander Scriabin unexpectedly died in the spring of

1915, Rakhmaninov broke with his custom of only playing his own works. He dedicated a series of concerts to his colleague's memory. This must have puzzled his audiences, because his interpretations were different from those they were used to from the composer himself. Both men believed in a close, reciprocal relationship between composing and piano playing and these memorial concerts once again underlined the contrast between them, raising doubts about Rakhmaninov's playing even in the minds of those who were not supporters of Scriabin. The composer Anatoly Alexandrov remembered: 'The only time I was unhappy with Rakhmaninov's playing was in a concert of some of Scriabin's works . . . shortly after his death. Admittedly there were some good points, for instance the elegant execution of the F-sharp minor Prelude op 11. I remember particularly well the inimitably graceful *rubato* in the final bars but his account of Scriabin's more significant works such as the Second and Fifth

The fabricated rivalry between Rakhmaninov and Scriabin (1872–1915) titillated audiences and critics alike. Although Rakhmaninov harboured some reservations concerning the harmonic and theosophical elements of Scriabin's progressive late music, he nonetheless considered him to be a very special case – not to be lumped together with the modernists he so loathed. Scriabin's tragic early death moved him to give a series of benefit concerts for Scriabin's widow.

Over the last decade of his life, Scriabin worked on his apocalyptic Mysterium, unrealised at his death, where he was attempting a unification of all the senses into a religious manifesto of his own devising, all to be performed at an Indian temple.

Scriabin's music attracted considerable critical success during his lifetime. His pianistic gifts were also greatly admired and ideally suited to the allure of his music. He was generously assisted by the unfailing support of his publisher, Belayev, and then later, Koussevitsky, who famously featured Scriabin in concerts on his chartered boat tours down the Volga.

Sonatas and the D-sharp minor Étude op 8 seemed to me very odd and entirely out of keeping with the spirit of the composer . . . I was especially shocked by Rakhmaninov's interpretation of the D-sharp minor Étude; he played it with enormous power and vigour but as a result he entirely lost sight of Scriabin's unique 'ecstatic' tension. I understood then that Scriabin's playing perfectly fitted that characteristic of his music which demands no actual power but the evocation of it.'[77]

> He plays everything in one single, really very beautiful, but terribly lyrical voice, indeed like all of his music. In this tone there is so much substance, so much meat, like on a prime cut of beef.
>
> Alexander Scriabin on Rakhmaninov. From Leonid Sabaneyev, *Memories of Scriabin*, Moscow 1925

The death of Sergey Taneyev a few weeks later was a great loss to Rakhmaninov, who wrote an obituary for the *Russian News*: *On 6 June Sergey Ivanovich Taneyev died unexpectedly – a master composer, the most cultivated musician of his generation, a man of rare individuality, originality and spiritual quality and the quintessence of musical Moscow . . . For all of us who knew him and visited him he was the ultimate arbiter, possessing wisdom, a sense of justice, intelligence and simplicity. He was exemplary in everything he put his hand to, for whatever he did he did well. Through his personal example he taught us how to live, to think, to work and even to speak – that is, to speak in his own idiosyncratic way: briefly, succinctly and clearly . . . We all valued his advice and guidance highly because we had faith in them and that faith came from our confidence that the advice he gave was always good.*[78]

The period starting in the autumn of 1917 was marked by uncertainty and unrest; concerts and journeys were affected by the war and worry about day-to-day survival. To this was added the effort to maintain the musical infrastructure of performances, management and publishing.

A meeting between Rakhmaninov and Sergey Prokofiev at one of the Scriabin memorial concerts at the end of 1915 proved significant. The young Prokofiev was unimpressed by the protests of Scriabin's disciples and liked Rakhmaninov's exceptionally clear and accomplished playing. After the concert he went straight to the dressing-room: '"You played very well all the same, Sergey Vassilievich." Rakhmaninov smiled wryly: *But you no doubt thought that I played badly?* he replied and turned away. Thenceforth good relationships ceased, certainly in no small measure because he rejected my music which made him angry and irritated.'[79] Rakhmaninov had no time for the 'wild' Prokofiev; in his capacity as consultant to the Russian Music Publishing House he did his best to block publication of the problematic *Scythian Suite*. He could not follow this music and all he heard was its barbaric and cacophonous components. It had been the same with Igor Stravinsky's *Rite of Spring*; this trend went against the grain with him, although with the years he came to understand its musical qualities and importance. In America their paths crossed occasionally but contact between them remained cool and distant.

At about this time the voice of a young singer and actress, Nina Koshets (1894–1965) and her charm and youthful naturalness made an impression on Rakhmaninov. They began giving recitals together, in which their performance of his Songs op 34 was particularly acclaimed. In the late summer of 1916, this collaboration inspired the composer to write his last song cycle, the eight Songs op 38, which he dedicated to the young singer.

I think that Rakhmaninov's music contains certain melodic phrases which are typical of him and extraordinarily beautiful. There are not many, and once one has found them one keeps meeting them again in other compositions of his.
Sergey Prokofiev on Rakhmaninov. From *Prokofiev über Prokofiev: Aus der Jugend eines Komponisten*, ed David H Appel, Munich 1981

Marietta Shaginian wrote in her Memoirs: 'He really did not think much of the symbolists but I still tried to make him find something he could value in them.'[80]

She did so with some suc-
cess, as witness the Songs
op 38, all the texts of
which (mostly love
lyrics) are by contempo-
rary 'symbolist' poets.
Though their range of
poetic imagery and mood
is very wide, even dis-
parate, the musical set-
ting is stylistically homogeneous. Compared with
the earlier song cycles,
this music is less open
and direct and more
stylised, in keeping with
the modern texts – for
example, the impression-
istic, flickering accompa-
niments to nos 1, 3 and 5
and the prevalence of a
kind of musical finely
chiselled drawing in

Nina Koshets' voice and charm impressed both
Rakhmaninov and Sergey Prokofiev

place of heavy oil-painting. This is his most modern cycle, not
only in the choice of texts; above all, declared the critics,
Rakhmaninov had been true to himself: 'The composer's approach
to his task – the musical reincarnation of new images and forms –
was, it seems, perfectly correct. He did not begin by following in
the footsteps of those who are perhaps organically connected and
closer to the new poetry (as others did) but by searching in his
own soul for the impetus capable of responding of its own accord
to even the very newest poetry.'[81]

Rakhmaninov himself thought the most successful of the Songs were *Daisies* (no 3) and *The Rat-catcher* (no 4)[82] – two inspired pieces in which character and mood are clearly contrasted.

Daisies, to a poem by Igor Severianin, recalls the cheerfulness and bright, pellucid pastel shades of earlier songs such as *Lilac* (op 21, no 5), *It is lovely here* (op 21, no 7) and *At my window* (op 26, no 10), yet its interplay of text and music is here more delicately crafted. He opens with the melody in the piano, to which the voice contributes a recitative 'textual accompaniment'. Only in the reprise, when the daisy is revealed as a symbol of the female sex, does the vocal line take up the cantilena. The piano leads throughout, in strange contrast to the original title 'Poem for voice with piano'. It was appropriate that the composer should later transcribe it as a piano solo; the melody emerges strongly and more compellingly than in the case of *Lilac*. *Daisies* was later popularised by another Russian émigré, the virtuoso violinist, Jascha Heifetz, in his own transcription.

The Rat-catcher, to a poem by Valery Bryusov (inspired by Goethe's ballad of the same name), is a kind of scherzo – an unusual mood for a Rakhmaninov song. It starts with a 'rogue motif' which reveals new characteristics each time it recurs. A spirited panorama unfolds, a rare demonstration of Rakhmaninov's gift for irony and ambiguity. It hints at the 'Mephisto Theme' of the First Piano Sonata but also at the diabolic element latent in the later Paganini Rhapsody. The subject of both works is the enchantment of music, through the *Rat-catcher*'s flute and Paganini's violin. Here the subject is treated more directly than in *Daisies* and this simplicity and monothematic development make the song exceptionally vivid, almost theatrical.

The premiere of the Songs confirmed these impressions. 'The focus of the evening [with the singer Madame Koshets and the composer at the piano] was the accompanist – not simply *de jure* as the creator of everything that was played, but also *de facto* as a miraculous, incomparable artist who gives his music flesh and blood and sets it on fire with the breath of life. This breath permeated the whole atmosphere of the performance. Rakhmaninov's playing was not just an accompaniment to the singing but was like a sort of creative foundry, out of which Vulcan's storms were kindled and delicate intricacies emerged, in the face of which the singing became less important and derivative.'[83]

The concerts with Nina Koshets were no more than a shaft of light in the darkening economic and political situation in Russia. The hope which Rakhmaninov had invested in the March Revolution came to nothing. The rouble fell rapidly, food was scarce and wounded soldiers were to be seen everywhere. Uprisings had begun in rural areas and when the Rakhmaninovs went to Ivanovka in early summer reliable accounts of assaults on property-owners and innocent civilians were rife. Fearing the worst, Rakhmaninov considered selling Ivanovka. Their situation was precarious: he had no prospect of earning money through concerts or in any other way and attempts to obtain engagements in the neutral Scandinavian countries yielded only the faintest hope. The family left Ivanovka early and spent the rest of the summer in the Crimea. They lived through the October Revolution anxiously huddled in their Moscow flat. Meanwhile local government had ceased to function, the electricity supply was cut off, and looting was a daily occurrence.

In these circumstances Rakhmaninov did not hesitate when he received an invitation to Sweden. Preparations for the journey quickly made and he hurried to St Petersburg, followed shortly afterwards by his family. Only one cousin saw them off: 'A gloomy autumn evening in Petrograd. The Finland Station. The platform . . . In front of the carriage Rakhmaninov stands with his family. He is leaving Russia. Once again I am seeing him off, now for the last time . . . A final farewell – scant anguish and tears . . . The third signal for departure . . . He kisses me and climbs into the

Тов. Ленин ОЧИЩАЕТ
землю от нечисти.

Revolutionary Poster: Conrade Lenin sweeps the
world clean of all filth

carriage. The train has stolen away . . . Leaving was hard for him
. . . Especially during his last years he was overwhelmingly
haunted . . . by a huge, active longing for his native land . . . He
dreamt of returning home, but died in a foreign country.'[84]

Abroad (1918–1943)

Rakhmaninov described his departure from Russia in these stark terms: *They invited me to Stockholm for ten concerts. The invitation was not very interesting; at any other time I might not have accepted it. I sent a telegram, got my visa . . . and even left with thoughts of success.*[85]

The Rakhmaninovs only stayed a few days in Stockholm and then went on to Denmark, where Russian friends helped them take their first steps as emigrants. A flat was rented for them in a suburb of Copenhagen and Rakhmaninov at once started preparing for his forthcoming concerts. The Scandinavian performances alleviated their immediate financial need but offered no future, as concert tours further afield in Europe were out of the question because of the war. In the late summer of 1918 he received several offers from America, including a 25-concert tour and conducting engagements in Cincinnati and Boston. The invitation to work with the renowned Boston Symphony Orchestra was attractive but he did not want the strain of conducting over a hundred concerts in thirty weeks, with no free time to study scores carefully. Also, his English was poor, he had only a passing acquaintance with the country, and bad memories of his tour in

In April, 1918, the Boston Symphony began its search for a new conductor to replace Karl Muck. The board of the symphony first approached Ossip Gabsilovich, the distinguished pianist, conductor and former pupil of Leschetizky. In an astonishing act of magnanimity, Gabsilovich suggested the newly exiled Rakhmaninov might be a more worthy choice! After considering the Boston offer, which proposed 110 concerts in thirty weeks, Rakhmaninov declined, fearing there would be insufficient time to prepare the repertoire or rehearse the orchestra properly.

1909. In his position, refusing both offers would have needed courage, though he did not want to commit himself for a long period. He decided to go to America.

Friends and admirers helped pay for the voyage, including among them the pianist Ignaz Friedman, who gave him 2000 dollars. Just as the Rakhmaninovs landed in New York the First World War ended. Soon old friends turned up: the violinists Fritz Kreisler and Efrem Zimbalist and his fellow pianist Josef Hofmann. Hofmann recommended him to his agent Charles Ellis of Boston, with whom he signed a contract and agreed on 36 concerts in 15 towns in the current season, the first being a recital on 8 December. Rakhmaninov was very happy with Ellis's management and never regretted this decision.

Rakhmaninov's decision to pursue a career as a pianist was not dictated by outward pressures but carefully considered; he preferred to develop himself as an instrumentalist rather than shackle himself to an orchestral institution. His conducting ability was well known in America, and he could easily have become director of one of the famous American orchestras. In 1924 the position of chief conductor of the Boston Symphony Orchestra fell vacant and his name was put forward, but Sergey Koussevitzky was given the post, apparently because his wealthy wife donated a substantial sum of money to the

Austrian by birth, the violinist Fritz Kreisler (1875–1962) was also the composer of a String Quartet, the operetta, *Apple Blossoms* and numerous cadenzas and short character pieces which continue to grace the violin repertoire. Rakhmaninov paid tribute to his great friend by transcribing two of his most famous works, *Liebesleid* and *Liebesfreud*, resulting in these highly elaborate and contrapuntally ingenious transformations, complete with cadenzas and bravura variations which foreshadow the writing to follow in the Paganini Rhapsody. The duo partnership of Rakhmaninov and Kreisler produced some of the most remarkable sonata recordings in history.

orchestra. 'One might think that this manoeuvre of the Koussevitzkys would have been a blow to Rakhmaninov's American career but . . . it was a blessing in disguise. There are many conductors but only one Rakhmaninov. Once he became a music director, Rakhmaninov would most certainly have cut back his piano playing. And the members of the BSO board would have driven him crazy with their opinions on budget and repertoire. So it was better for music that Rakhmaninov continued actively performing as a pianist.'[86]

The United States never won Rakhmaninov's affection. He respected the country and its people but the hectic bustle and transitory relationships upset him; he never came to terms with them. He could not feel at home in America, because he came to know it as a traveller, rushing from one concert to another. Also, he was extremely shy and his thoughts and hopes always lay with Russia and Europe. He learnt to understand the language and could eventually follow radio and television broadcasts without difficulty, but his English was never fluent. Both his private letters and business correspondence had to be translated for him. He was proverbially monosyllabic and shunned all unnecessary social intercourse, which heightened the impression he gave of being a somewhat aloof foreigner. He abhorred the receptions, banquets and socialising beloved of Americans and refused virtually all invitations. Ironically, people grew accustomed to his ways; the more eccentric he seemed, the more his reputation as an artist grew.[87] In the grip of a serious illness he naturally had a presentiment of his approaching end. In order to protect his family from any complications about the rights to his legacy, he made the enormous sacrifice of taking American citizenship.[88]

Unlike the majority of Russians who left their country because of the October Revolution and the upheavals of the Civil War, Rakhmaninov quickly and effortlessly found his feet financially in America. This enabled him to maintain and even outstrip the

Rakhmaninov in 1934

upper-middle-class lifestyle of the 'belle époque,' with servants, cook, chauffeur and secretary. However, he was a modest man and treated his retainers unaffectedly and without condescension. He made few demands for himself and would happily have foregone most of the comforts he thought important for his family, but he did allow himself some luxuries, such as suits from the best English tailors[89] and – to satisfy his passion for motoring – the best, most expensive and newest models of cars.[90]

Characteristically, most Russian emigrants found it hard to get used to new living conditions and preferred to keep to themselves, showing little inclination to integrate. Their pride in their nationality was only accentuated by the wretched conditions in which most of them were living. Rakhmaninov could afford to cultivate his Russianness in his immediate surroundings, as few other emigrants could. He only really felt at home among other compatriots and therefore liked to surround himself with them. Almost all his servants were Russian, even though this was frequently inconvenient and caused him difficulties with language and problems over passports and visas for his frequent foreign trips. The food in his house was Russian and 'In a word, Sergey Vassilievich always preferred anything which bore the Russian imprint.'[91] When he had time to read, he read Russian literature, especially his favourite author Chekhov, whom he had met in his youth. He also enjoyed contemporary Russian memoirs and historical works. He did not much like new Russian fiction, finding most of it artificial and conceited. Although he could read German, English and French, he preferred translations and even Shakespeare, whom he loved, he only read in Russian.[92]

Rakhmaninov's success on the concert platform was certainly not only due to his outstanding gifts as a pianist and to good management, but also to his charisma, his distinctive physical presence and a modicum of luck and chance, for the circumstances were not conducive for even a top-class virtuoso pianist to establish himself in America. All his efforts to help other prominent Russian pianists to get engagements there were fruitless. In 1922 he wrote: *Look at Nikolay Medtner, for example; I have been trying for nearly two years to get him an engagement with any impresario but all in vain.*[93] And three years later, when Matvey Presman was under the illusion that he could settle in America with Rakhmaninov's help, the latter wrote to him: *You will doubtless agree with me that Alexander Ziloti has a very good name and even recommendations from the late Franz Liszt, but none of this saved him from having to teach, or in other words, from needing money.*[94]

Rakhmaninov and Josef Hofmann were the two most highly paid pianists of their time. At the height of the Depression, when the breadwinner of a family would count himself lucky to earn 3000 dollars a year and a five-course meal in a restaurant cost one dollar 25, Rakhmaninov was earning about 135,000 dollars.

Harold C. Schonberg,
The Virtuosi, New York 1985

Rakhmaninov became one of the most sought-after and best-paid pianists in the United States and could decide how often he wanted to perform without worrying about money. He could have given many more or many fewer concerts. He was hard hit by the 1931 Depression and lost all of his capital that was in shares and other investments, but this caused him no hardship, unlike the humiliation suffered by other people. 'Rakhmaninov had good business sense and was always investing in various enterprises. Of course, he had business advisers. Every artist who makes good money is besieged by people with advice on how to invest it. But Rakhmaninov found the time and patience to sort out the advice and to act accordingly, which made him rather an exception.'[95]

Rakhmaninov's success was due to a whole range of fortunate attributes: great musical gifts, theatricality, large, mobile hands and the ability to work in a consistent and disciplined manner. He knew that he could not make a living by only playing his own works, so at the age of 45 he set to work to build up a new repertoire and perfect his technique. At first he practised for about five hours a day and later, when he felt more confident, he cut this down to three or four hours.

More important than the length of time were the concentration and self-discipline with which he practised – never just the works he was about to perform but also a whole range of exercises. He admired the studies of Karl Czerny and Charles Hanon. 'Before concerts he almost always played Hanon exercises in all the keys

Rakhmaninov's
hands
photograph by
Eric Schaal

and in a variety of rhythmic arrangements, then two or three of Karl Czerny's Études from op 74 – and that was it. He loved Czerny's studies, saying that their unusually good and clever design made them ideal for technical finger exercises.'[97] Even in the late twenties, long after he had stopped needing to fight for recognition, he was careful to keep up his technique. He would play difficult passages extremely slowly, so that anyone hearing him would think he was a student rather than the great pianist.[98] 'Rakhmaninov played his exercises very slowly and any diligent pupil would cheer up to hear how slowly the great pianist practised and what painstaking attention he paid to every note and the work of every finger. Once from another room I heard him playing like that and although every detail of the piece was familiar to me I could not recognise Liszt's *Waldesrauschen*.'[99]

There is too little evidence to allow one to reconstruct Rakhmaninov's system of practising, but his rule was definitely to practise with the greatest intensity, as though under performance conditions. 'After working . . . his face was serious and stern (like in a concert).'[100] Demanding pieces he worked at passage by passage. 'Once he was learning Liszt's *La Campanella*, going through separate passages. I was surprised at his patience. He literally repeated the same passage ten times, meticulously polishing it. Regardless of the fact that he never played the whole piece through but limited himself to repeating certain difficult passages, I was struck by the beauty of the sound.'[101]

Rakhmaninov knew that physical presence and charisma were two vital prerequisites for a pianist's success. He once said that the public mainly went to concerts to see artists in the flesh,[102] but he did not play to the gallery or show off. His striking appearance (which led the press to speculate repeatedly whether he had Asiatic blood), his disciplined, controlled bearing, his thrilling musicality and technical mastery all blended into a fascinating synthesis of extraordinary, spellbinding power.

There is no doubt that Rakhmaninov compiled his recital programmes with an astute eye to what would interest and appeal to
audiences. His taste was broadly in line with that of the general
public. He had no missionary zeal for any particular artistic trend
or composer and unobtrusively included works of his own, and
occasionally compositions by Nikolay Medtner, Alexander
Scriabin or Sergey Taneyev as well. Variety and a deliberate mixture of style and period characterised the content of these programmes. They usually began with either baroque works – by J S
Bach, or possibly Handel, Domenico Scarlatti, or Couperin, sometimes in arrangements by Busoni, Leopold Godowsky or Karl
Tausig – or Viennese classics by Haydn, Mozart or Beethoven, and
occasionally a mixture of the two. The 'centre of gravity' was
always the great romantics: Schumann, Chopin, Liszt, more rarely
Schubert or Weber (both usually in Tausig's arrangements),
Mendelssohn or Grieg. He would then finish with some highly
virtuoso items.

He rejected 'unpianistic' compositions which ran counter to the
instrument's character, including works by Brahms and Rimsky-
Korsakov.[103] Modern and contemporary music was only occasionally included in his programmes – works by Debussy, for instance,
or Scriabin, but never the latter's bold later compositions. He said
about Scriabin's Fifth Piano Sonata: *An exceptionally beautiful work
but a little too modern to meet my taste entirely.*[104]

In orchestral concerts Rakhmaninov usually played either his
Second or Third Piano Concerto, according to the impresario's
wishes. In later years he would have preferred to play his First or
Fourth Concerto, or the Paganini Rhapsody more often, but he
really liked the Third Concerto best: *With my own concertos I much
prefer the third, because my second is uncomfortable to play and therefore
not susceptible of equally successful effects.*[105]

Rakhmaninov the pianist is commonly taken as belonging to
the tradition of Liszt and Anton Rubinstein, but his yardstick was

in fact Chopin's style of playing rather than Liszt's.
Chopin's pianism was for
him the fundamental criterion of how to play the
instrument, and he recom-
mended it at every possible
opportunity. *It seems somewhat*
astonishing that since the time of
Chopin no master has arisen to
enrich the literature of the piano
in such a magnificent manner.
With all due respect for Liszt,
whose works form such a very
important step in the advance of
pianistic art, Chopin still
remains at the zenith. His

Frédéric Chopin portrait by Eugène Delacroix,
1838, Louvre, Paris

exquisite sense of tone colour, his gorgeous harmonies and his always
pianistic realisation of the possibilities of the keyboard, make his works a
kind of Bible for pianists.[106]

Only after the end of the 1930s did he occasionally play con-
certos by other composers again – Beethoven's First Piano
Concerto (*music fit for the gods!*[107]), Schumann's Piano Concerto and
Liszt's *Totentanz*.

Rakhmaninov was brought up in the spirit of Liszt's approach
to piano technique, especially by Ziloti who absolutely idolised
him, but his playing was equally shaped by the conservative, clas-
sically-minded Moscow School through Taneyev, who was sceptical of Liszt's methods to the point of hostility. These conflicting
influences were not however irreconcilable. Anton Rubinstein had
admired Liszt as a performer but attacked him as a composer,
starting a battle which became all the fiercer as the composers of
the New Russian School, such as Balakirev, Borodin and

Mussorgsky, came to his defence. Rubinstein was the first to introduce a critical attitude to Liszt into the circles of conservative Russian musicians and this attitude had its effect on Rakhmaninov. For them it was Chopin who authentically carried on the classical tradition – Liszt, on the contrary, had destroyed it. It would, of course, be unhelpful to play Rakhmaninov off against Liszt; he clearly illustrates the ideas of the New German School and profited directly from Liszt's pianistic innovation. On the other hand he obviously felt a greater debt to Chopin.

Rakhmaninov portrait by Sergey Somov, 1925

One must emphasise that Rakhmaninov always understood Chopin in a markedly modern sense and particularly protested against his being regarded as a salon composer. *With regard to Chopin there is in these days a tendency which I have observed among certain musical artists. They cite the letters of Chopin and the statements of his contemporaries to prove that he had little strength and that therefore he played everything mezza voce, delicately, never fortissimo. And it follows, they say, that all his compositions should be played in a subdued manner, with delicacy but never robustly. This opinion is not sympathetic to me. I do not understand Chopin's music thus. Behind me and behind all the artists who play Chopin in the 'grand manner', the broader style, stands Rubinstein. He could play in all styles; he could have played Chopin in the subdued style if he had liked. But he did not choose to play it that way.*[108]

One example of this modern style of interpreting Chopin is Rakhmaninov's unsentimental approach to the B-flat minor Sonata op 35. In fact, all his interpretations and recitals were marked by their modernity: the programme, its cohesion and relative brevity (under 90 minutes actual playing-time) but finally and essentially the style of the concert. The American music critic Harold Schonberg put it like this: 'All his playing had extreme musical elegance, the melodic lines shaped with ineffable authority. It possessed a manly, aristocratic kind of poetry hard to describe; without ever becoming sentimental, Rakhmaninov managed to wring dry the emotional essence of his music. He did it by a kind of subtly nuanced phrasing within his strong, clear, unfussy projection of the lines . . . His playing was marked by definition; where other pianists became blurry through abuse of the pedal, or deficiencies of finger, Rakhmaninov's textures were crystalline . . . It took some years for this kind of playing to become the model for the new generation of pianists. Rakhmaninov's brilliance, of course, was immediately recognized.'[109]

Rakhmaninov could unquestionably have won greater success and public acclaim if he had been more willing to accept the media of radio and recordings. Radio in particular he disliked . . . *to my mind, radio has a bad influence on art: that it destroys all the soul and true significance of art. To me it seems that the modern gramophone and modern methods of recording are musically superior to wireless transmission in every way, particularly where reproduction of the piano is concerned.*[110] His scepticism was not only due to the technical shortcomings of early radio, but also to the 'modern' way of listening to radio distractedly, which he hated because it banished music to the back of the listener's mind.

It is doubtful whether Rakhmaninov appreciated the importance of recording, apart from its commercial aspect which certainly interested him. He was essentially a 19th-century artist, in that he preferred the concert experience and the 'live' impact of music to any form of artificial reproduction. The finality and arbitrariness of reproducing an existing interpretation made him uneasy and he did not belong among those artists who – depending on their success and standing – cooperated fully with the recording industry and made it serve their principles and ideas. *I get very nervous when I am recording . . . When the test records are made, I know that I can hear them played back to me, and then everything is all right. But when the stage is set for the final recording and I realise that this will remain for good, I get nervous and my hands get tense.*[111]

Ampico and Duo-Art Piano Rolls were just two of the many competing systems of reproducing piano music popular at the turn of the century. These recording systems should not be confused with mere mechanical pianos, which had very limited dynamic subtleties and were used to churn out thousands of popular song arrangements. This new technology achieved unparalleled levels of expression, rhythmic nuance, and pedal sensitivity and eventually attracted the greatest pianists of the times to record their performances for posterity. Artists as diverse as Gershwin, Hofmann, and Paderewski all jumped on the recording bandwagon.

Rakhmaninov was no exception. Displaying his usual interest in technological innovations, he positively endorsed the results of his test recordings and famously remarked after hearing a playback of his G minor Prelude: *Gentlemen, I have just heard myself play.*

Rakhmaninov made even greater demands when recording than when performing. He fell upon even the tiniest rough patches and either refused to release a recording or re-recorded it, which is possibly why he left relatively few records and was rarely completely happy even with them. 'He often said that the records he made served him as an excellent lesson and demonstration of what he should avoid when performing. Sergey Vassilievich would detect in his playing something which did not satisfy him or a mannerism of which he had previously been unaware.'[112]

When he was living in America, Rakhmaninov always longed for the 'old' world, and as soon as he could arrange it he was per-forming again in Europe, initially only sporadically in the 1920s but there-after regularly. From 1928 on he divided the concert season as evenly as he could between Europe and America. This was also for his family's sake, espe-cially for his daughters, to whom he wanted to give a comprehensive education and an international cul-tural life. France was the obvious focal point; in the period between the wars Paris was the undisputed centre for Russian emi-

Rakhmaninov with his granddaughter Sophia Wolkonsky, 1930

grants, where just about every known aspect of Russian culture, science and politics was to be found.

Irina (1903–1969), his elder daughter, married into the Russian aristocratic family of the Wolkonskys. Her husband, Count Peter Wolkonsky, died a year after their marriage and she and her daughter, who was born in 1925, remained very close to her par-ents. Tatyana (1907–1961), the younger of the two, married into the well-known and widespread family of Russian musicians called Konyus. They originally came from France where their name was Conus. She settled in Paris with her husband Boris and son Alexander and remained there throughout the Nazi occupation, to her father's great anxiety.

Almost all Rakhmaninov's leisure activities centred around the interests and pleasures of his family – the summers spent in Paris, in Normandy and on the Italian Riviera, journeys to Florence, Cannes and Dresden, where Natalya's family, the Satins, had settled. Even the visit he paid to the Bayreuth Festival in 1932 was probably arranged as a concession to the family and not because he particularly wanted to go.

The Villa Senar on Lake Lucerne. Rakhmaninov's modernism expressed in his choice of architecture

Rakhmaninov helped many Russian immigrants who were in straitened circumstances – unobtrusively and without asking for anything in return. In 1925, to support Russian culture in exile and also to give his daughters something to do, he founded Tair Publishers – named after them: Ta for Tatyana; ir for Irina. Its publications included new Russian music, including his four Piano Concertos, and contemporary Russian literature by writers such as Alexey Remisov. Tair also published a monograph on Sergey Taneyev, commissioned from the music critic Leonid Sabaneyev,[113] in spite of the fact that in Russia he had harshly criticised Rakhmaninov. The latter was above bearing a grudge when he had an opportunity to help a gifted musician who had fallen on hard times through no fault of his own.

Rakhmaninov practising at the Villa Senar

The summers in particular brought on Rakhmaninov's feeling of homelessness and he looked back sadly on the holidays at Ivanovka. The longer he lived in the West, the more he yearned for a refuge for calm and reflection. The family argued for a long time over where to make a new home, the daughters pleading for France, the father for Germany. They finally agreed on Switzerland, where Rakhmaninov bought a plot of land in an idyllic situation at Hertenstein, on the shores of Lake Lucerne. There he built a large modern villa with every imaginable comfort and called it Senar (Se for Sergey; na for Natalya; r for Rakhmaninov). The plans and their execution swallowed up enormous sums of money, but he spared no expense when it was a question of re-creating a piece of homeland. In Senar, where he spent each summer up to and including 1939, he did in fact feel at home and adopted the place as a 'second Ivanovka'.

At Senar Rakhmaninov was finally able to gather together his inner forces and compose again. To this end he withdrew for days on end, worked round the clock and would speak to nobody. He exchanged few words even with the family and never talked about the nature or progress of his work. Each new composition grew out of an agonising process. When it was completed he felt a great inner sense of release.

Rakhmaninov was an enthusiastic motorist; for instance, he loved to drive from Paris to Senar in a day. He also enjoyed lengthy motorboat trips on Lake Lucerne, showing a youthful delight in the mechanics of his boat allied with a sporting competitiveness – a trait which can occasionally be discerned in his piano-playing.

Rakhmaninov in his motorboat Senar on Lake Lucerne

After leaving Russia, Rakhmaninov composed relatively little – six works in all, plus some revisions of earlier compositions and a number of piano transcriptions of other composers' works for concert performance.

It may well have been less the obvious burden of concert tours than a feeling of spiritual emptiness and rootlessness which held him back from composing: *For when I left Russia, I left behind me my desire to compose: losing my country, I lost myself also. To the exile whose musical roots, traditions and background have been annihi-*

lated, there remains no desire for self-expression; no solace apart from the unbroken and unbreakable silence of his memories.[114]

In 1917 Rakhmaninov had already made a sketch for a Fourth Piano Concerto, but not until the spring of 1926 did he succeed in completing the work, in the space of a few months, during the first long interval between concerts he allowed himself in 1925/6, after eight years of uninterrupted touring.

The musical language of the Fourth Piano Concerto goes well beyond its predecessors. The melodic sweep of the first movement is more intense, the harmonies harsher, the tone colours darker. Heroic gestures fall repeatedly into melancholy brooding and its overall expression is more bitter and pessimistic. Some features belong to the 1920s:

Rakhmaninov with his grandchildren Sophia Wolkonsky and Alexander Konyus in Switzerland

rhythms inspired by jazz, more transparent structure, almost like chamber music, and more succinct formal layout. The last movement may be thought long-winded, but Rakhmaninov certainly was not the only composer to struggle with the problem of how to finish a work. It is no weaker than the last movement of the Third Concerto and perhaps surpasses it in nervous tension and daemonic fire. Apparently George Gershwin admired it (and for his part Rakhmaninov was an admirer of Gershwin).

Rakhmaninov feared that the concerto would meet with sceptical reactions but even he was surprised at the vehemence of a few of his critics. Not satisfied with it himself, he revised it in 1927 and again, more thoroughly, in 1940 and it has since then usually been played in this last version.

In November 1926, only a few months after completing the

Fourth Concerto, Rakhmaninov composed another work, Three Russian Songs for mixed choir and orchestra, which is still little known today. Although these songs are based on genuine Russian folk tunes, they are not folk compositions in the narrow sense; they are less arrangements than meditations inspired by folk melodies. On the other hand it is remarkable to find Rakhmaninov, who had until then avoided borrowing directly from folk music, here openly doing so. In spite of the apparently playful subject, a sorrowful and melancholy tone predominates the work and the Songs can be interpreted as an attempt to give artistic expression to grief over a lost homeland and feelings of yearning and nostalgia. There is a studio recording of an arrangement of the third song, entitled *A Russian Folk Song,* made in February 1926 with the mezzo-soprano Nadezhda Plevitskaya and the composer at the piano. Although he was anything but a nationalist composer, Rakhmaninov saw himself as Russian by origin and character – not in the sense of artistic ideology but as a self-evident and natural definition.

In my own compositions, no conscious effort has been made to be original, or romantic, or nationalistic, or anything else . . . I am a Russian composer, and the land of my birth has influenced my temperament and outlook. My music is the product of my temperament, and so it is Russian music; I never consciously attempted to write Russian music.

Rakhmaninov in an interview with *The Étude,* Philadelphia, Dec 1941

While not a highly cultured person, Rakhmaninov was a man of wide interests and hated intellectual pomposity or showmanship. Contacts with Russian emigrant culture, especially in Paris, were important to him primarily for his daughters' sake; he himself remained aloof and preferred not to become involved in anything outside his own field. He did, however, cling with heartfelt, almost nostalgic, emotion to old friendships from his Moscow days – mostly musicians he knew as a student and in his early years as a conductor – whereas his relationships with people he met after 1917 were generally more distant and formal. He did not take the initiative in communicating with other people but confined himself to contact with close family and friends, and deliberately shut himself away from the outside world because his unmistakable appearance made him easily recognisable.

When Fyodor Chaliapin visited him in the early 1920s with friends from the Moscow Art Theatre, Rakhmaninov's habitual gloom lifted; he relished the singer's risqué jokes with almost childlike delight. Chaliapin counted as a member of the family – a musician friend from early years, a man of sparkling wit and anything but an intellectual.

Rakhmaninov found it hard to come to terms with contemporary developments in composition and when interviewed, said so: *My taste is very conservative. I do not like modernism.*[115] In a letter to Nikolay Medtner he divided composers into three categories: *1) those who write popular music, that is, for the market, 2) those who write fashionable, so-called modern, music and finally 3) those who write 'serious, very serious music'*,[116] and put himself and Medtner into the last category. This distinction is not very convincing, particularly when it puts 'fashionable' and 'modern' music together. It is also not clear what he actually means by the 'moderns'. To him everything is 'modern' which does not speak directly from the heart. If he had mentioned names or works it would have been easier to analyse his meaning. The musicians of the Viennese School, such as Schoenberg, Berg and Webern, and neo-classicists such as Stravinsky would not have appealed to him but on the

After Medtner's artistically and financially successful tour of America in 1932, he arrived home in Europe only to find that his cheque for $2,500.00 from the American promoter had bounced. Swindled, distraught and on the brink of collapse, Medtner's wife wrote to Rakhmaninov for assistance in procuring legal advice in New York. Instead, Rakhmaninov magnanimously paid Medtner's entire fee out of his own pocket.

other hand 'modern' trends do appear in his own works, in spite of his declared traditionalism.

Because Rakhmaninov was a man of few words who set no store by the discussion of aesthetics, his comments on the 'moderns' should be treated with caution. Medtner's aversion to them was more ideologically motivated, rooted in his desire to resolve aesthetic questions and conflicts in principle. In his case an element of bitterness also came into it, because he was relatively unsuccessful as either composer or pianist. Although he tried repeatedly to enlist Rakhmaninov as an active supporter of his cause, he never succeeded. In fact the latter did always agree with him both fundamentally and in general terms, but often just to avoid irritating and pointless debate. Their relationship gradually became strained: Medtner considered Rakhmaninov's Third Symphony excessively 'modern'.

In the 1930s Rakhmaninov wrote two sets of variations: in 1931 the Corelli Variations op 42 and in 1934 the Paganini Rhapsody op 43. The former was his first work in that form to surpass the Chopin Variations in essential content, and the piano part is simpler and more transparent. The theme is not actually by Arcangelo Corelli but is based on an old Iberian folk tune traditionally known as 'Les Folies d'Espagne' or 'La Folia' which Rakhmaninov came across in the final movement of Corelli's Violin Sonata op 5, no 12, through his fruitful collaboration with Fritz Kreisler.[117] In the 1920s Rakhmaninov had already immortalised the famous violinist's Viennese genre pieces *Liebesleid* and *Liebesfreud* in his virtuoso arrangements for piano. The reference to Corelli is no coincidence; his melancholy clarity has unmistakable affinity with Rakhmaninov's own demeanour. The écoles variations only wreath themselves around the theme which later undergoes changes in tone colour, harmony and melody and assumes new forms, first as a minuet and then as a chorale enveloped in the sound of bells. In the middle are two quiet variations in the major key, followed by livelier scherzo episodes out of which grows a thrilling finale. The work ends in a deliberately anti-virtuoso coda, with calm and peaceful echoes of the theme.

Rakhmaninov often played the Corelli Variations in public but was over-critical of himself and never satisfied with his performance, even giving up the idea of recording it. He put much of his experience with this work into the Paganini Rhapsody, which resembles it in both ideas and structure. He chose a familiar theme (the final section of Paganini's 24 Caprices op 1, on which Brahms and Liszt had already written variations), planned the sequence of variations as a sonata and used a similar technique in formulating the variations. This is one of comparatively few compositions in variation form for piano and orchestra, together with Liszt's *Totentanz* (which Rakhmaninov greatly admired) and César Franck's Symphonic Variations. The Rhapsody was to be his last work in piano concerto form and his last for solo piano.

The Rhapsody quickly became one of the most popular and most frequently played of all Rakhmaninov's works. In 1937 the Russian-born choreographer Mikhail Fokine suggested mounting it as a ballet,[118] and when Rakhmaninov heard about this he immediately thought of a scenario. It gives a unique insight into his 're-creative' imagination: *Should one not revive the legend of Paganini selling his soul to the devil in return for perfection in his music-making and also for women? All the variants on the* Dies Irae *theme are the devil and the whole of the middle section (variations 11 to 18) contain love-stories. Paganini appears in the theme itself (his first appearance) and for the last time, when vanquished, in the first 12 bars of variation 23. There follows till the end the exultation of the conqueror. The devil first appears in variation 7 and the passage at figure 19 could be a dialogue with Paganini, as his theme blends here with the* Dies Irae. *Variations 8 to 10 show the development of the devil. Variation 11 is the transition into the realm of love; from variation 12 (the minuet) to variation 18, the woman appears for the first time. In variation 13 we see*

Paganini's first encounter with women; variation 19 is the celebration of Paganini's art – his diabolical pizzicato. It would be useful to see Paganini with a violin – not a real one, of course, but something dreamt-up, fantastical. What's more, it occurs to me that at the end of the piece a few of the representatives of evil in the struggle for women and art should bear a caricatured, absolutely ludicrous resemblance to Paganini himself. They too should have violins here, but even more fantastically grotesque ones.[119]

The medieval plainchant, *Dies Irae* (*Day of Wrath*), has fascinated composers for generations. While Berlioz and Liszt famously incorporated the theme in *Symphonie Fantastique* and *Totentanz*, Rakhmaninov was repeatedly drawn to this motto, and used it in *The Isle of the Dead,* Études-Tableaux op 39, the Symphonic Dances and, most ingeniously, in the Paganini Rhapsody. Though many commentators attributed Rakhmaninov's incessant use of the *Dies Irae* to a morbid obsession, it is more likely that Rakhmaninov enjoyed the compositional opportunities afforded in this theme, as well its threatening undertow.

Musicologists have produced evidence of Rakhmaninov's repeated use of the *Dies Irae* theme from the Catholic requiem mass – in the *Isle of the Dead, The Bells,* the Rhapsody, the Third Symphony and the Symphonic Dances – but have not proved whether he consciously alludes to it in any of these works. Since his tunes are usually spun out as sequences from small melodic phrases, they often come involuntarily close to the generic *Dies Irae* theme, or indeed render it literally, without necessarily being deliberate quotations or even allusions (although they can always be deciphered as such). Anglo-American scholars could be criticised for obsessively making the *Dies Irae* theme the focal point of their analysis and for being blind to the nuances involved.[120]

The last two works – the Third Symphony op 44 and the Symphonic Dances op 45 – faithfully continue along the trail which their composer had already blazed. Here are similarly sharpened contrasts in thematic working and harmony, the instrumentation is more varied and new and unexpected colour effects are developed. Although long stretches of the Third Symphony sound free and rhapsodic, the thematic material and structure are actually strictly developed. All the movements are suffused with a melody evoking archaic folk song and setting the inner emotional and thematic focus. The sonata structure is reduced to three movements, as the slow movement (*adagio*) and the scherzo (*allegro vivace*) are merged into one.

The Third Symphony can be regarded as Rakhmaninov's last decisive step towards achieving international recognition as a composer, even though after finishing the Second Symphony he had unequivocally asserted that he would *never compose another symphony . . . I shall not be able to but the important thing is that I don't feel like writing one*.[121] The Third Symphony is among the few works of his which he liked. With his usual reserve he said: *Personally I am firmly convinced that it is good. But . . . even composers sometimes get it wrong! Be that as it may, I have stuck firmly to my opinion to this day*.[122] Two years later he was revising this work too.

He composed Symphonic Dances in the clear knowledge that it would be his last work. It is remarkable, and untypical of him, that they refer back to earlier works: the main theme from the First Symphony and the sound of Russian Orthodox hymns which he used in *Vespers*. So these Dances can be regarded as a conclusion, a synthesis, a last attempt to create a memorial to his lost homeland, as mirrored in his own works. The original subtitles to the movements ('morning,' 'midday' and 'twilight') he later replaced with the even more sombre 'midday,' 'twilight' and 'midnight' – an expression of his dour outlook on life. (*I am by nature a pessimist.* [123])

In parallel with the orchestral version, Rakhmaninov wrote one for two pianos, which he and Vladimir Horovitz often played together at his home on Long Island and later in Beverly Hills.

As usual, the Rakhmaninovs had spent the summer of 1939 at Senar. The political situation was dire but they could only guess that this might be their last summer in Europe. Soon after they had returned to America for the new season, this foreboding was to become a tragic certainty.

At first life in America continued as usual, but after the war reached France and Russia no one could any longer entertain illusions about the future. The Rakhmaninovs realised that they had lost their home for the second time and that America, the country they loved little, would now have to offer them protection and a living.

Rakhmaninov had never completely relinquished his contacts with Russia. In the hard winter of 1922/3 during the Civil War he had sent money and food parcels to friends and acquaintances, and supported various artistic enterprises in Moscow, Leningrad (as it then was), Kiev and Kharkov as well as publishing and researching projects. From the late 1920s on he was again in contact with friends from his Conservatory days, such as Alexander Goldenweiser, Alexander Gödicke, Nikita Morosov and Reinhold Glière.

In the 1930s, however, these contacts suffered a setback. On 15 January 1931 the Circle of Russian Culture published an article in the *New York Times*, challenging the rumour which had spread in the West that the Soviet Union was creating a model system of education. Instead it deplored the ideological terror of a 'Communist gang, numerically decreasing but well-organised'.[124] Rakhmaninov was one of the signatories. Immediately the Soviet press heaped opprobrium on him and he found his works unofficially banned until 1933. Even thereafter his music remained out of favour and was not performed for 'ideological reasons' – *Vespers*, because of its religious content and *The Bells* for its literary sym-

Rakhmaninov's last home, 610 Elm Drive, Beverly Hills, Los Angeles

bolism. The sound of bells (that is, monastery bells) was considered to embody a seditious spirit in conflict with the might of the Soviet state.

But all this was forgotten as Russia was plunged into war in 1940. To the end Rakhmaninov followed the news from the front with intense interest. He felt himself bound to Russia as never before and even gave a benefit concert for the Soviet army.

Once again he was looking for a new 'home', first on Long Island, where he composed the Symphonic Dances in the summer of 1940, and finally in Beverly Hills in California, because of its more agreeable climate. There in 1942 he made his first and only appointment to meet Stravinsky privately. So as to avoid argument, they did not talk about music (Rakhmaninov only admired Stravinsky's early work). Their common ground was their worry about Russia and about family and friends living in France.[125]

Constant travelling and the strain of giving concerts had already left their mark on Rakhmaninov in the 1930s and had necessitated treatment in Baden-Baden and Aix-les-Bains, but now in America his strength was failing fast. He felt under pressure and spiritually restless and had to resist his addiction to coffee and cigarettes. He looked like a shadow of his former self and was always feeling weak and tired. Out of a sense of duty he gave his last concerts in February 1943 – superbly, as always. The doctors initially diagnosed pleurisy and neuralgia, then cancer. The end came quickly; he died on 18 March 1943, a few days before his seventieth birthday.

The music of Igor Stravinsky (1882–1971) towered over the 20th century artistic climate, sending shockwaves around the world and sounding the death knell of Rakhmaninov's epoch. Stravinsky's long career spanned many notable artistic transformations and reinventions, from the epic Russian ballets, *Firebird*, *Petrushka*, *The Rite of Spring* and *Les Noces*, to his neo-classical period initiated by his work on *Pulcinella*. Astonishingly, Rakhmaninov actually adored *Petrushka* and *The Firebird*, declaring them works of genius and truly Russian in the greatest sense. During the outbreak of the Second World War, both men found themselves living nearby in California and with similar worries – chiefly,

that their children were stranded in wartime France. Through an intermediary, Rakhmaninov sent Stravinsky an invitation to dinner, Stravinsky jumped at the chance and the two composers finally met.

Rakhmaninov had put in his will that he wanted to be buried in the Novodevichy Cemetery in Moscow, where Alexander Scriabin, Sergey Taneyev and Anton Chekhov had found their last resting-places, but as he was an American citizen this was not possible and he was buried in the Kensico Cemetery near New York.

What will remain of Rakhmaninov? So far as one can predict, his works for piano and orchestra, a range of piano pieces and songs (which are still largely neglected in the West) and also the *Vespers,* which have only recently received due recognition anywhere.

His recordings will remain, too, and be perhaps all the more appreciated as the music market is flooded with waves of glossy and meaningless interpretations, which will make genuinely great and individual interpretations increasingly important, even if they are only available in historical recordings.

For Rakhmaninov musical greatness consisted in melody: *Melodic inventiveness is, in the highest sense of the term, the vital goal of the composer. If he is unable to make melodies which command the right to endure he has little reason to proceed with his studies in musical composition.*[126] He was a true Romantic who, in the teeth of all radical aesthetic change, insisted on authentic lyricism, which was already being denounced as antiquated. This was in fact the guarantee of his music's individualistic power and appeal and its survival to the present day.

When the American Walter Koons invited various musicians to

> An essential lyricism, so strikingly pronounced in all Russian music, is brought to the foreground in Rakhmaninov. Along with Glinka, Tchaikowsky and Borodin he was a brilliant melodist, gifted with the ability to create unusual themes of great beauty and emotional plenitude, distinguished by a bewitching versatility, freedom and breadth of inspiration.
>
> Yury Keldysh,
> *Rakhmaninov and His Time*, 1976

Sergey Rakhmaninov, Photograph by Eric Schaal, 1941

give a definition of music, Rakhmaninov's reply was typically brief and concise, couched in a few poetic words whose unguarded frankness seem as characteristic of the man himself as of his music: *What is music? It is a peaceful moonlit night; it is the rustling of living leaves; it is the distant evening bell; it is that which is born of the heart and pierces the heart; it is love! The sister of music is poetry but its mother is a heavy heart!*[127]

C. Рахманиновъ

Notes

1   Soya Arkadyevna Pribytkova, *Sergey Rakhmaninov in St Petersburg*. In *Vospominaniya o Rakhmaninove {Recollections of Rakhmaninov}*, ed Tsaruy Apetyan (hereafter *Recollections*), vol 2, 5th (amended) edition, Moscow 1988, p 55

2   Quoted from Marietta Shaginian, *Memories of Sergey Rakhmaninov*. In *Recollections*, vol 2, p 141

3   From a letter to Natalya Skalon, 7 Feb 1893 (old calendar, hereafter o c). In *Sergey Rakhmaninov. Literaturnoe nasledie / SR's Literary Legacy*, ed Tsaruy Apetyan (hereafter *Legacy*), vol 1, Moscow 1978, p 211

4   Marietta Shaginian, p 141

5   Sophia Satina, *Notes on Sergey Rakhmaninov* (hereafter Satina). In *Recollections*, vol 1, p 15

6   Anna Trubnikova, *Sergey Rakhmaninov*. In *Recollections*, vol 1, p 116

7   Sergey Bertensson & Jay Leyda (with Sophia Satina), *Sergey Rakhmaninov. A Lifetime in Music* (hereafter Bertensson/Leyda), New York 1956, p 3

8   Alfred J & Katherine Swan, *Rakhmaninov: Personal Reminiscences*. In *The Musical Quarterly* no. 2/1944, p 181/2

9   Matvey Presman, *A Small Corner in Musical Moscow in the '80s* (hereafter Presman). In *Recollections*, vol 1, p 158

10   Presman, p 157

11   Presman, p 156

12   Bertensson/Leyda, p 11

13   From an interview in *The Étude*, April 1932, p 239/40

14   Presman, p 156

15   Presman, p 303

16   Cf Satina, p 21

17   *Sergey Rakhmaninov, Memories*. In *Legacy*, vol 1, pp 52/3

18   Ludmila Rostovtsova (née Skalon), *Memories of Sergey Rakhmaninov*. In *Recollections*, vol 1, p 247

19 Alexander Ossovsky, *Sergey Rakhmaninov*. In *Recollections*, vol 2, p 346

20 Alexander Pushkin, *The Gypsy*. From Pushkin's *Works* ed Arthur Luther, vol 2, Leipzig 1923, p 222

21 Semyon Kruglikov. Quoted from Yuri Keldysh, *Rakhmaninov's Opera Debut*. In *Sovetskaya musyka* no. 8/1970, p 69

22 Bertensson/Leyda, p 55

23 Diary entry, 28 Nov 1898 (o c). From *Sergej Taneyev – Musikgelehrter und Komponist / Sergey Taneyev – Musicologist and Composer*, ed Andreas Wehrmeyer, Berlin 1996, p 176

24 Satina, p 28

25 Maria Chelistsheva, *Sergey Rakhmaninov in St Mary's School*. In *Recollections* , vol 1, p 386

26 Rostovtsova, p 242

27 From a letter to Boris Asafyev, 13 April 1917. In *Legacy*, vol 2, Moscow 1980, p 101

28 Cf *Rakhmaninoff's Recollections told to Oskar Riesemann*, (hereafter *R's Recollections*), Allen & Unwin, London 1934, p 55

29 From a letter to Natalya Skalon, 7 February 1893 (o c). In *Legacy*, vol 1, p 211/2

30 From a review in the *Moskovskye vedomosti / Moscow Gazette*. Quoted from Olga Sokolova, *Sergey Rakhmaninov*, Moscow 1984, pp 49/50

31 Yelena Somova, *Recollections*. In *Recollections*, vol 2, p 233

32 Quoted from Somova, p 233

33 Bertensson/Leyda, p 89

34 *Moskovskye vedomosti / Moscow Gazette*, 4 December 1900 (o c). Quoted from Yuri Keldysh, *Rakhmaninov i yevo vremya / Rakhmaninov and his Times*, Moscow 1973, p 170

35 Diary entry, 26 Oct 1901 (o c). From: *Sergej Tanejev* ed Wehrmeyer, p 179

36 Cf Letter to Marietta Shaginian of 8 May 1912 (o c). In *Legacy*, vol 2, p 48

37 Yelena Chukovskaya (née Kreizer), *Recollections of my teacher and friend Sergey Rakhmaninov*. In *Recollections* vol 1, pp 311/12

38 Natalya Rakhmaninova, *Sergey Rakhmaninova* (hereafter Rakhmaninova). In *Memories,* vol 2, pp 293/4

39 cf Rakhmaninova, p 316

40 *Moskovskye vedomosti / Moscow Gazette*, 5 September 1904 (o c). Quoted from Keldysh, p 211

41 From *How Russian Students Work* in *The Étude*, May 1923

42 Alexander Goldenweiser, *My Memories of Sergey Rachmaninov*. In *Recollections*, vol 1, p 422

43 Cf Nikolay Medtner, *Sergey Rachmaninov*. In *Recollections*, vol 2, p 351

44 From the interview: *The Composer as Interpreter*. In *The Monthly Musical Record*, Nov 1934

45 *Russkye vedomosti / Russian Gazette*, 14 Jan 1906 (o c). Quoted from Keldysh, p 226

46 Cf Shukovskaya, p 287

47 Rachmaninova, pp 294/5

48 From a letter to Mikhail Slonov, 21 Nov 1906 (Dresden). In *Legacy*, vol 1, p 408

49 From a letter to Nikita Morosov, 9 Nov 1906 (Dresden). In *Legacy*, vol 1, pp 404/5

50 From a letter to Nikita Morosov, 11 Feb 1907 (Dresden). In *Legacy* vol 1, p 423

51 Quoted from Keldysh, p 308

52 Quoted from Bertensson/Leyda, p 156

53 From a letter to Leopold Stokovsky, 20 April 1925. In *Legacy,* vol 2, p 167

54 From a letter to Nikita Morosov, 8 May 1907 (Dresden). In *Legacy*, vol 1, pp 433/4

55 Konstatin Igumnov, quoted from Keldysh, p 321

56 From a letter to Sergey Taneyev, 3 March 1909 (Dresden). In *Legacy* vol 1, p 472

57 From a letter to Joseph Yasser, 30 April 1935. In *Legacy*, vol 3, p 49

58 Vladimir Horovitz, quoted from the CD booklet for RCA Victor Red Seal 09026615642: *Sergey Rachmaninov, Third Piano Concerto.* Vladimir Horovitz, piano, with the New York Philharmonic Orchestra, conductor Eugene Ormandy

59 From an interview in *The Delineator* Feb 1910. Quoted from Bertensson/Leyda, p 162

60 *Rakhmaninov's Recollections*, pp 158/9

61 From an interview in *Musykalny truzhenik / Musical Worker* no 7/1910. In *Legacy*, vol 1, p 66

62 Review in *Utro Russiy (Morning in Russia)* 7 April 1910 (o c). Quoted from Keldysh, p 297

63 From *Scriabin and Rachmaninov*, in *Musyka* no 160/1913

64 Review in *Zhisn iskusstva / Artistic Life* no 51/1923

65 Rachmaninova, p 304

66 Alexander Osovsky, pp 373/4

67 Christoph Flamm, *Der russische Komponist Nikolay Medtner,* Berlin 1995

68 Marietta Shaginian, pp 116/17

69 From a letter to Marietta Shaginian 9 May 1912 (o c). In *Legacy* vol 2, pp 47/8

70 From a letter to Marietta Shaginian 15 March 1912 (o c). In *Legacy* vol 2, p 43

71 Bertensson/Leyda, pp 184/5 (extracts)

72 Alfred J and Katherine Swan, *Rakhmaninov: Personal Reminiscences.* In *The Musical Quarterly* no 1/1944, p 8

73 Bertensson/Leyda, p 369

74 bertensson/Leyda, p 263

75 Cf letter to Joseph Yasser, 30 April 1935. In *Legacy* vol 3, p 49

76 *Rakhmaninov's Recollections*, p 177

77 Anatoly Alexandrov, *My Meetings with Sergey Rachmaninov.* In *Recollections*, vol 1, pp 162/3

78 First published in *Russkie vedomosti / Russian Gazette,* 16 July 1915 (o c). Quoted from *Legacy* vol 1, p 68

79 *Sergey Prokofiev: Materialy, docoumenty, vospominania / Material, Documents, Memoirs,* ed Semyon Schlifstein, Moscow 1956, pp 35/6

80 Marietta Shaginian, p 120

81 Yuly Engel, *Sergey Rachmaninov and Nina Koshitz in Concert.* In Yu D Engel, *Glazami sovremennika / Through the eyes of a contemporary,* ed I Kunin, Moscow 1971, p 439

82 According to Marietta Shaginian, p 153

83 Yuly Engel, *Sergey Rachmaninov and Nina Koshitz in Concert*, p 438

84 Pribytkova, pp 88/9

85 From an interview in *Poslednie novosti / Latest News*, Paris, 30 April 1933. Quoted from *Legacy*, vol 1, p 125

86 Nathan Milstein & Solomon Volkov, *From Russia to the West*, London 1990, p 113

87 Cf Satina, p 67

88 Cf Rachmaninova, p 327 (and *Note* by Apetyan, p 522)

89 Cf Satina, p 68

90 Cf Nikolay Mandrovsky, *Memoirs*. In *Recollections,* vol 2, p 243

91 Satina, p 63

92 Cf Satina, p 69

93 From a letter to Reinhold Glière, 3 April 1922. In *Legacy*, vol 2, p 121

94 From a letter to Matvey Presman, 24 April 1925. In *Legacy* vol 2, p 168

95 Milstein/Volkov, p 115

96 Quotation from Barrie Martyn, *Rakhmaninov – Composer, Pianist, Conductor*, Scolar Press, Aldershot 1990, p 396

97 Pribytkova, p 60

98 Irina Chaliapina, *In memoriam Sergey Rachmaninov*. In *Recollections*, vol 2, p 177

99 Arthur Hirst, *Memoirs*. In *Recollections*, vol 2, p 345

100 Mikhail Chekhov, *Memoirs*. In *Recollections*, vol 2, p 286

101 Yury Nikolsky, *From my Memories*. In *Recollections*, vol 2, p 50

102 Cf interview in *The Musical Observer*, May 1927

103 Cf interview *How Russian Students Work* in *The Étude,* May 1923

104 *The Musical Observer*, April 1921

105 *The Étude*, May 1923

106 *The Étude*, May 1923

107 From a letter to Vladimir Vilshau, 7 June 1937. In *Legacy*, vol 3, p 110

108 From the interview *Interpretation Depends on Talent and Personality* in *The Étude,* April 1932

109 Harold Schonberg, *The Great Pianists,* New York 1985, pp 316/17

110 From an interview with *The Gramophone*, April 1931

111 Quoted from Alfred J and Katherine Swan, *Rakhmaninov: Personal Reminiscences.* In *The Musical Quarterly*, no 1/1944, p 11

112 Satina, p 109

113 Refers to the work *S I Taneyev*, Paris 1930. The book did not conform to the ideas of Rakhmaninov, who had expected something

more in the style of Sabaneyev's *Recollections of Scriabin*, Moscow 1925, i e, a literary documentary of authentic narrative and more or less literal quotations.

114 From the interview *The Composer as Interpreter*. In *The Monthly Musical Record*, Nov 1934

115 *Poslednie novosti {Latest News}*, 30 April 1933. Quoted from *Legacy*, vol 1, p 125

116 From a letter to Nikolay Medtner, 14 Jan 1925. In *Legacy*, vol 2, p 184

117 Fritz Kreisler and Sergey Rakhmaninov also made several recordings together

118 The premiere of Mikhail Fokine's ballet *Paganini* with music by Rakhmaninov took place on 20 July 1939 at Covent Garden Opera House, London

119 From a letter to Mikhail Fokine, 29 August 1937. In *Legacy*, vol 3, p 114

120 This reproach could, for instance, also be levelled at Barrie Martyn's work *Rakhmaninov – Composer, Pianist, Conductor*, London 1990

121 From a letter to Nikita Morosov, 13 April 1907 (Dresden). In *Legacy*, vol 1, p 4331

122 From a letter to Vladimir Vilshau, 7 June 1937. In *Legacy*, vol 3, pp 1099/10

123 From an interview with *The Gramophone*, April 1931

124 Cf Victor Seroff, *Rakhmaninov*, New York 1950, p 178

125 Cf Sergey Bertensson, *Memoirs*. In *Recollections,* vol 2, p 282

126 *The Étude*, Oct 1919

127 Quoted from the Russian original in Sophia Satina, *S V Rachmaninov* in *Muzykalnaya Akademia* no 2/1993, p 208

Chronology

Year	Age	Life
1873	0	Sergey Vassilievich Rakhmaninov born on 20 March old calendar (1 April new calendar), son of Vassily Arkadievich Rakhmaninov and his wife Lyubov Petrovna née Butakov at their estate of Semyonov, south of Lake Ilmen. The family moves to the estate of Oneg, north of Novgorod.
1877	4	First piano lessons.
1882	9	The family moves to St Petersburg. Studies at St Petersburg Conservatory.
1885/6	12	Piano lessons in Moscow with Nikolay Zverev, who also takes responsibility for his education. Enters Moscow Conservatory.
1886	12	January/February, attends Anton Rubinstein's Historical Concerts.
1887	14	First attempts at composition.
from 1888	15	Piano tuition with Alexander Ziloti, theory and composition with Anton Arensky and Sergey Taneyev.
1890	17	Starts working on First Piano Concerto.
1891/2	18/9	Diploma in piano and composition from Moscow Conservatory.
1893	20	27 April, premiere of opera *Aleko* at Bolshoi Theatre.
1897	23/4	15 March, failure of First Symphony at its premiere in St Petersburg, resulting in creativity crisis. Autumn, appointed conductor at private Mamontov Opera, Moscow. Meets Fyodor Chaliapin.
1898	25	September, travels with Mamontov Opera to Crimea. Meets Anton Chekhov.
1899	26	April, first overseas concert appearance in London, as conductor and pianist.

Year	History	Culture
1873	In Spain, Amadeo I abdicates; republic proclaimed. In Africa, Ashanti War begins (until 1874). In Asia, Acheh War (until 1903). Great Depression (until 1896).	Arthur Rimbaud, *A Season in Hell*. Walter Pater, *Studies in the History of the Renaissance*. Claude Monet, *Impression: soleil levant*.
1877	Queen Victoria proclaimed Empress of India. Russo-Turkish War.	Émile Zola, *L'Assommoir*.
1885	Belgium's King Leopold II establishes Independent Congo State. In Transvaal, gold discovered.	Zola, *Germinal*. Guy de Maupassant, *Bel Ami*.
1886	In Cuba, slavery abolished. In India, first meeting of National Congress.	H Rider Haggard, *King Solomon's Mines*.
1887	In Britain, Queen Victoria celebrates Golden Jubilee.	Verdi, *Otello*.
1888	In Germany, William II becomes emperor (until 1918). In Asia, French Indo-China established.	N Rimsky-Korsakov, *Scheherezade* op 35. Edward Bellamy, *Looking Backwards*.
1890	In Germany, Otto von Bismarck dismissed. In Spain, universal suffrage.	Tchaikovsky, *The Queen of Spades*. Paul Cézanne, *The Cardplayers*.
1891	Building of Trans-Siberian railway begins. Shearers' strike in Australia.	Tchaikovsky, *The Nutcracker*. Oscar Wilde, *The Picture of Dorian Gray*.
1893	Franco-Russian alliance signed. France annexes Laos.	Dvořák, *From the New World*. Tchaikovsky, *Pathétique*.
1897	In Britain, Queen Victoria celebrates Diamond Jubilee. Britain destroys Benin City. Klondike gold rush (until 1899).	Joseph Conrad, *The Nigger of the Narcissus*. Stefan George, *Das Jahr der Seele*. Strindberg, *Inferno*. Edmond Rostand, *Cyrano de Bergerac*.
1898	Spanish-American War: Spain loses Cuba, Puerto Rico and the Philippines. Britain conquers Sudan.	Henry James, *The Turn of the Screw*. H G Wells, *The War of the Worlds*. Zola, *J'Accuse*.
1899	Second Boer War (until 1902). Aspirin introduced.	Hector Berlioz, *The Taking of Troy*. Edward Elgar, *Enigma Variations*.

Year	Age	Life
1900	26	January to April, treatment from neurologist Dr Nikolay Dahl, who succeeds in restoring his self-confidence. Starts work on Second Piano Concerto.
1901	28	27 October premiere of Second Piano Concerto op 18, conducted by Alexander Ziloti, Moscow.
1902	29	29 April, marries his cousin Natalya Alexandrovna Satina. Honeymoon, visit to Bayreuth Festival. December, performances of Second Piano Concerto in Vienna and Prague.
1903	30	Finishes Variations on a theme by Chopin op 22 and Preludes op 23. Birth of his daughter Irina.
1904	31	Engaged as conductor at Bolshoi Theatre. Also conducts symphony concerts.
1905	32	Joins other musicians in signing resolution demanding basic citizens' rights in Russia.
1906	32/3	11 January, world premiere of one-act operas *The Miserly Knight* op 24 and *Francesca da Rimini* op 25. June, relinquishes duties as conductor at Bolshoi Theatre. Spends winter months (also 1907 and 1908) in Dresden. Begins work on the Second Symphony.
1907	34	26 May, pianist and conductor in Russian Symphony Concert in Paris. Finishes Second Symphony op 27 and First Piano Sonata op 28. Birth of his daughter Tatyana.
1908	34	26 January, conducts world premiere of Second Symphony in St Petersburg.
1908/9	35	First performances in Germany (2 December and 23 January, Berlin; 18 December, Frankfurt-am-Main), playing piano part in Trio op 19 and Second Piano Concerto.
1909	36	Spring, finishes *The Isle of the Dead* op 29 in Dresden. Nominated Vice-President of Russian Music Society. Summer months, composes Third Piano Concerto op 30.
1909/10	36/7	November to January, American tour. 28 November, world premiere of Third Piano Concerto in New York, conducted by Walter Damrosch. 16 January, further performance under Gustav Mahler. Composes Preludes op 32.
1911	38	Composes Études-Tableaux op 33.

1900 First Pan-African Conference.
In France, Dreyfus pardoned.
Relief of Mafeking.
In China, Boxer Rebellion (until 1901).

Puccini, *Tosca*.
Conrad, *Lord Jim*.
Sigmund Freud, *The Interpretation of Dreams*.

1901 In Britain, Queen Victoria dies; Edward VII becomes king.
Theodore Roosevelt becomes president.

Strindberg, *The Dance of Death*. Freud, *The Psychopathology of Everyday Life*.
Anton Chekhov, *The Three Sisters*.

1902 Peace of Vereeniging ends Boer War.
Anglo-Japanese alliance.

Debussy, *Pelléas et Mélisande*.
Scott Joplin, *The Entertainer*.
Hillaire Belloc, *The Path to Rome*.

1903 Bolshevik-Menshevik split in Communist Party of Russia.
In Russia, pogroms against Jews.

Henry James, *The Ambassadors*.

1904 France and Britain sign Entente Cordiale.
Russo-Japanese War.
Photoelectric cell invented.

Puccini, *Madama Butterfly*.
Chekhov, *The Cherry Orchard*.

1905 Russian revolution against monarchy fails.
Bloody Sunday massacre.
Korea becomes protectorate of Japan.

Richard Strauss, *Salome*.
Albert Einstein, *Special Theory of Relativity*.

1906 Algeciras Conference resolves dispute between France and Germany over Morocco.
Duma created in Russia.
Revolution in Iran.

Henri Matisse, *Bonheur de vivre*.
Maxim Gorky, *The Mother*

1907 Anglo-Russian Entente.
Electric washing-machine invented.

Conrad, *The Secret Agent*.
Rainer Maria Rilke, *Neue Gedichte*.

1908 Bulgaria becomes independent.
Austria-Hungary annexes Bosnia-Herzegovina.

Gustav Mahler, *Das Lied von der Erde* (until 1909).
E M Forster, *A Room with a View*.

1909 In Britain, pensions begin.
In Britain, Lloyd George's 'People's Budget' is rejected by House of Lords; causes constitutional crisis.
Congo Free State under direct rule by Belgian parliament.
In Turkey, Young Turk revolution.
In Nicaragua, US supports revolution.

Strauss, *Elektra*.
Rabindranath Tagore, *Gitanjali*.
Sergey Diaghilev forms Les Ballets Russes.
F T Marinetti publishes manifesto of Futurism in *Le Figaro*.

1910 George V becomes King of Britain.
Union of South Africa created.
Japan annexes Korea.

Constantin Brancusi, *La Muse endormie*.
Igor Stravinsky, *The Firebird*.
Forster, *Howard's End*.
Bertrand Russell, *Principia mathematica*.

1911 Chinese revolution against imperial dynasties.

Strauss, *Der Rosenkavalier*.

Year	Age	Life
1912	39	Correspondence with Marietta Shaginian. Composes Songs op 34. Conductor of Moscow Philharmonic Society.
1913	40	In Rome composes cantata *The Bells* op 35. Second Piano Sonata op 36.
1915	41/2	January/February, completes *Vespers (All-night Vigil)* op 37; 10 March, world premiere under Nikolay Danilin. 14 April, death of Alexander Scriabin; 6 June, death of Sergey Taneyev.
1916	43	Songs op 38.
1917	44	Completes Études-Tableaux op 39. 5 September, last concert in Russia (Yalta). October Revolution and subsequent chaos. Accepts invitation to Sweden. December, Rakhmaninovs leave Russia for good.
1918	44/5	Concerts in Scandinavia. Decides on career as pianist. Leaves for USA. 8 December, first recital in Providence, Rhode Island.
1920	47	Recording contract with Victor Talking Machine Company.
1921	48	Buys house in New York.
1922	49	First European post-war concerts (piano recitals), London.
1923	50	Meets Fyodor Chaliapin and members of the Moscow Art Theatre.
1926	52/3	Stops giving concerts for one year. Composes Fourth Piano Concerto op 40 and Three Russian Songs op 41.
1927	53	18 March, world premiere of Fourth Piano Concerto and Three Russian Songs in Philadelphia under Leopold Stokowski.
1930	57	Buys plot of land in Hertenstein/Weggis on Lake Lucerne. Builds magnificent villa andnames it Senar.
1931	57	Signs article in *New York Times* of 12 January, harshly criticising Soviet cultural policies. Polemical reaction against him in Soviet press and boycott of his works in Soviet Union until 1933. Variations on a Theme by Corelli op 42
1934	61	Rhapsody on a Theme by Paganini op 43. 7 November, premiere with Philadelphia Orchestra in Baltimore under Leopold Stokowski.
1936	63	Completion of Third Symphony op 44. 6 November, world premiere in Philadelphia under Leopold Stokowski.

1912	Balkan Wars (until 1913). ANC formed in South Africa. Titanic sinks.	Arnold Schoenberg, *Pierrot lunaire*. Carl Jung, *The Psychology of the Unconscious*.
1913	In US, Woodrow Wilson becomes president (until 1921).	Stravinsky, *The Rite of Spring*. Marcel Proust, *À la recherche du temps perdu*
1915	Dardanelles/Gallipoli campaign (until 1916). Italy denounces its Triple Alliance with Germany and Austria-Hungary. In Britain, Women's Institute founded.	Ezra Pound, *Cathay*. Marcel Duchamp, *The Large Glass* or *The Bride Stripped Bare by her Bachelors, Even* (until 1923).
1916	Battle of Somme. Battle of Jutland.	Guillaume Apollinaire, *Le poète assassiné*. G B Shaw, *Pygmalion*.
1917	In Russia, revolutions in February and October. Tsar Nicholas II abdicates. Communists seize power under Vladimir Lenin.	First recording of New Orleans jazz. Franz Kafka, *Metamorphosis*. Giorgio de Chirico, *Le Grand Métaphysique*.
1918	Treaty of Brest-Litovsk between Russia and the Central Powers. In Russia, Tsar Nicholas II and family executed.	Oswald Spengler, *The Decline of the West*, Volume 1. Paul Klee, *Gartenplan*.
1920	IRA formed. First meeting of League of Nations.	Edith Wharton, *The Age of Innocence*.
1921	National Economic Policy in Soviet Union.	Sergey Prokofiev, *The Love of Three Oranges*.
1922	Soviet Union formed. Benito Mussolini's Fascists march on Rome.	
1923	Vladimir Lenin dies.	Le Corbusier, *Vers une architecture*.
1926	Germany joins League of Nations. France establishes Republic of Lebanon. Hirohito becomes Emperor of Japan.	Puccini, *Turandot*. Kafka, *The Castle*.
1927	Joseph Stalin comes to power. Charles Lindbergh flies across Atlantic.	Martin Heidegger, *Being and Time*. Virginia Woolf, *To the Lighthouse*. BBC public radio launched.
1930	London Round-Table Conferences on India. Mahatma Gandhi leads Salt March in India. Frank Whittle patents turbo-jet engine.	W H Auden, *Poems*. T S Eliot, 'Ash Wednesday'. William Faulkner, *As I lay Dying*.
1931	King Alfonso XIII flees; Spanish republic formed. Ramsay MacDonald leads national coalition government in Britain. New Zealand becomes independent. Japan occupies Manchuria.	
1934	In Germany, the Night of the Long Knives. In China, the Long March. Enrico Fermi sets off first controlled nuclear reaction.	Dmitri Shostakovich, *Lady Macbeth of Mtsensk*. Agatha Christie, *Murder on the Orient Express*. Prokofiev, *Peter and the Wolf*.
1936	Germany occupies Rhineland. Edward VIII abdicates throne in Britain; George VI becomes king.	A J Ayer, *Language, Truth and Logic*. BBC public television founded.

Year	Age	Life
1939	66	11 August, last concert in Europe (Lucerne).
1941	67	3 January: world premiere of Symphonic Dances op 45 in Philadelphia under Eugene Ormandy.
1941/2	68/9	As well as existing concert commitments, gives two benefit concerts for the Soviet army. Buys house in Beverly Hills, California.
1943	69	17 February, cuts short season with final concert (Knoxville, Tennessee). 28 March, dies in Beverly Hills.

1939	Stalin and Hitler sign non-aggression pact. 1 September: Germany invades Poland.	Steinbeck, *The Grapes of Wrath*. John Ford, *Stagecoach* with John Wayne.
1941	Operation Barbarossa: Germany invades Soviet Union. Italians expelled from Somalia, Ethiopia and Eritrea. In US, Lend-Lease Bill passed. Churchill and F D Roosevelt sign Atlantic Charter. Japan attacks Pearl Harbor.	Bertolt Brecht, *Mother Courage and her Children*. Orson Welles, *Citizen Kane*.
1943	Allies bomb Germany. Battle of Kursk. Allies invade Italy: Mussolini deposed. Tehran Conference. Lebanon becomes independent.	Richard Rodgers and Oscar Hammerstein, *Oklahoma*. Jean-Paul Sartre, *Being and Nothingness*. T S Eliot, *Four Quartets*.

Bibliography

The following list is limited to a selection of the most important publications to date. Works of research in the narrower sense are not included. Further bibliographic information can be found in R Palmieri's Rakhmaninov Research guide (see below) and in Geoffrey Norris's article on Rakhmaninov in *The New Grove Dictionary of Music and Musicians* vol 15, London 1980 and Yuri Keldysh's article in *Musykalnaya Enciklopedia* vol 4, Moscow 1978.

Apetyan, Tsaruy Apetovna (ed): *S. Rakhmaninov. Literaturnoe nasledie / Literary Legacy*, vol 1-3, Moscow 1978/80.

Apetyan, Tsaruy Apetovna (ed): *Vospominania o Rakhmaninove / Memories of Rakhmaninov*, vol 1–2, 5th, enlarged edition, Moscow 1988.

Asafyev, Boris Vladimirovich: *Izbrannie trudy / Selected works*, vol 2, Moscow 1954, pp 289–311.

Bertensson, Sergei and Jay Leyda (with Sophia Satina): *Sergei Rakhmaninov. A Lifetime in music*, New York 1956.

Belyayev, Victor Mikhailovich: *S.V. Rakhmaninov*, Moscow 1924. Engl transl: in *The Musical Quarterly* no 3/1927, pp 359–76.

Biesold, Maria: *Sergei Rakhmaninov 1973–1943. Zwischen Moskau und New York (Between Moscow and New York)*, Berlin 1991.

Briankeva, Vera Nicolaevna: *S.V. Rakhmaninov*. Moscow 1976.

Jungheinrich, Hans-Klaus: Toteninsel als Ziel und Ausgangspunkt. Zur künstlerischen Physiognomie von Sergey Rakhmaninov. In *Piano-Jahrbuch* 1981, pp 70–75

Kandinsky, Aleksey Ivanovich: *S.V. Rakhmaninov (Album)*, Moscow 1988.

Keldysh, Yury Vsevolodovich: *Rakhmaninov I yevo vremya / Rakhmaninov and his time*, Moscow 1973, pp 426–35.

Keldysh: Der Schaffensweg von Sergej Rachmaninow, in *Kunst und Literatur*, no 10/1973, pp 1028–39.

Martyn, Barrie: *Rakhmaninov – composer, pianist, conductor*, London 1990.

Milstein, Nathan and Solomon Volkov: Rakhmaninov as I knew him, in *From Russia to the West*, London 1990, pp 106–25.

Norris, Geoffrey: *Rakhmaninov*, London 1976.

Norris, Geoffrey: Rakhmaninov's second thoughts, in *The Musical Times*, no 4/1973, pp 364–68

Palmieri, Robert: *Sergei Vasil'evich Rakhmaninov*. A guide to research, New York – London 1985.

Piggott, Patrick: *Rakhmaninov's orchestral music*, London 1974

Poivre d'Arvor, Catherine: *Rachmaninov ou la passion au bout des doigts / Rakhmaninov or passion at his fingertips*, Monaco 1986.

Riesemann, Oskar von: *Rakhmaninov's Recollections told to Oskar von Riesemann*, London 1934

Rubinstein, Arthur: *Mein glückliches Leben / My Many Years*, Engl transl: London 1980

Rüger, Christoph: Ein Künstler – zwei Leben. Zum 100. Geburtstag Sergei Rachmaninows, in *Musik und Gesellschaft* No 4/1973, pp 198–203

Sabaneyev, Leonid: Sergey Rakhmaninoff, in *Modern Russian composers*, New York 1927, pp 103–20

Schonberg, Harold C: *Skrjabin und Rakhmaninov in Die grossen Komponisten. Ihr Leben und Werk (Great composers. Their lives and works)*, Frankfurt-am-Main – Berlin 1986, pp 559–75

Seroff, Victor: *Rakhmaninov*, New York 1950

Sokolova, Olga Ivanovna: *Sergei Vassilevich Rakhmaninov*, Moscow 1984

Swan, Alfred J and Katherine: Rakhmaninov: Personal reminiscences, in *Musical Quarterly* nos 1& 2/1944

Threlfall, Robert: *Sergei Rakhmaninov. His life and music*, London 1973

Threlfall, Robert and Geoffrey Norris: *A catalogue of the compositions of S. Rakhmaninov*, London 1982

Walker, Robert: *Rakhmaninov. His life and times*, New York 1978

Translator's Note

I have in principle followed the Library of Congress system, but deviated
– consistently – from the exaggeratedly purist transliteration much in
vogue today, involving apostrophes for the Russian soft sign and use of
e with an umlaut and i with a line above it, which can only confuse an
English reader. It is nearly impossible to transliterate all Russian vowel
sounds accurately, seeing that some vary according to their position in
the word, but I have given the Russian 'e' as 'ye' and 'e umlaut' as 'yo',
including in proper names (although Russian artists called Yelena tend
to use Elena in the West), since this is the most accurate way of conveying the sound.

I have given the Russian diphthong vowels as 'ya' and 'yu', to convey
the softness of the first sound and also used 'y' at the end of words and
between vowels, for ease of reading. Where there is a well-known version of a proper name – eg Bolshoi, Chaliapin, Tchaikovsky – I have
retained it. (We have inherited the last two of these, together with many
others, from French, which has had a strong influence on traditional
transliteration from the Russian.)

I am indebted to Beatrice Kilroy for her help in translating many of
the Russian quotations and for the advice of several friends whose
knowledge of the language was greater than mine.

Anne Wyburd

Testimonials

BORIS ASAFYEV

Rakhmaninov's great success lies in his unsung melody. In this he doggedly stuck to his guns unaffected by theoretical reflections. His melody always evolves, like a path through fields, unpremeditated, uncontrollable. Whether motivated by verse, inspired by a symphonic design, or sung by the sensitive fingers of Rakhmaninov the pianist, one senses in it all the unbroken inspiration and the authenticity of the artist, engendered by a powerful, but deeply disciplined sentiment . . .

The firm melodic foundation on which the structure of Rakhmaninov's composition takes root had its origins in a singular sovereignty of the will and nobility of the soul. It was not wilfulness, but an unbending culture of sentiment, of music as the creed of mankind. In what was a difficult time for Russian art, the aesthetic refinements of its seductions could not force Rakhmaninov to turn away from his natural path. He suffered deeply from cruel accusations that he was old-fashioned, reactionary, belonged in the 'salon', but he did not give in, retaining in his marvellously artistic character his own ethos, his moral superiority – loyalty to his gift.

Sergey Rakhmaninov. In: *Recollections* vol 2, ed Z Apetyan, Moscow 1988, pp 383/4.

LEV MASEL

Rakhmaninov often combines the unmeditated, open, emotional lyricism of Tchaikovsky . . . with an element of particular ballast, a sustained immersion in a singular emotional and psychological state; with long periods of a more or less constant level of emotional tension. Rakhmaninov cultivated to a very high degree a means of communication through music, which fuses emotions such as aspiration, openness and rapture with a special, whole and vital peace. Related to this, for instance, is a distinctive brand of apprehending nature – peaceful, serene, but very intense and internally agitated – expressed in a way that Rakhmaninov alone was able to perfect. In terms of the fusion of dynamism with ballast, there exists another nuance specific to Rakhmaninov's brand of sentimentalism, consisting in the concentration of emotion to be communicated, which requires special attention and asserts the values of suffering. In those [frequent] instances where . . . Rakhmaninov's lyricism . . . asserts the strength and purity of sentiment, he underscores its independent value.

O melodiy / On melody, Moscow 1952, pp 269/70.

IVAN BUNIN

At my first meeting with him in Yalta, something occurred between us that had a good deal in common with the sort of thing that only happened in Herzen's and Turgenev's romantic youth, when young people could spend whole nights in conversation about how beautiful, eternal and superior art was . . . [The next time] our lives had already taken very different directions, fate had severed everything, our meetings were always accidental and increasingly brief and there was, it seemed to me, in general something in the character of my esteemed friend that was very reserved. But that first night we were still young, we were far removed from restraint . . . We went out on to the terrace, continuing a conversation about the fall from grace of prose and poetry then occurring in Russian literature. Without noticing it, we proceeded into the courtyard of the hotel, then on to the shore, to the pier . . . It was already late, there was not a soul anywhere. We sat down on some sort of cable which gave off the scent of tar and that special sort of freshness that you will only find by the Black Sea. We talked and we talked more and more passionately and joyfully about what we remembered with wonder from Pushkin, Lermontov, Tyutchev, Fet and Maykov.

Sergey Rakhmaninov. In *Recollections,* vol 2, ed Z Apetyan, Moscow 1988, p 25.

VICTOR BELYAYEV

. . . It was Rakhmaninov's fate to live in the midst of this multitude of jostling and divergent currents in contemporary Russian music, currents whose force was exerted in one of two directions – either towards the capture of new positions or towards the consolidation of those already won; to live at the moment of the tremendous rupture in the history of Russian music brought about by Scriabin, who rejected, so to speak, the age in which his contemporaries had their being. Furthermore, Rakhmaninov had to work under these conditions, asserting his creative individuality and moulding by his influence as a creator the life surrounding him. In this concourse of circumstances we see the reason for the profoundest tragedy of his work – the tragedy of a great soul expressing itself in language and by methods which were antiquated, whereas under other conditions they would have harmonized with the times.

S V Rakhmaninov. Kharacteristika yevo tvorcheskoy deyatelnosti I ocherk zhizni / S V Rakhmaninov. Description of his creative work and a summary of his life, Moscow 1924, p 4. (Quoted in *The Musical Quarterly no 13/1927, transl S W Pring.*)

ARTHUR RUBINSTEIN

Rakhmaninov was a pianist after my heart. He was superlative when he played his own music. A performance of his concertos could make you believe that they were the greatest masterpieces ever written, while when they were played by other pianists, even at their best, they became clearly what they were: brilliantly written pieces with their oriental languor, which have retained a great hold on the public. But when he played the music of other composers, he impressed me by the novelty and originality of his conceptions. When he played a Schumann or a Chopin, even if it was contrary to my own feelings, he could convince me by the sheer impact of his personality. He was the most fascinating pianist of them all since Busoni. He had the secret of the golden, living tone which comes from the heart and which is inimitable. In my strong opinion he was a greater pianist than a composer. I fall, I have to admit, under the charm of his compositions when I hear them but return home with a slight distaste for their too brazenly expressed sweetness.

My many years, Jonathan Cape, London 1980, pp 87/8.

NIKOLAY MEDTNER

What always struck me about Rakhmaninov was that every time one of his pieces was performed there was this beauty, the most genuine outpouring of beauty. This alone earns one's sympathy – that he is not ashamed or afraid to charge the music with beauty in such huge quantities.

From Marietta Shaginian, quoted in *Recollections* vol 2, ed Z Apetyan, Moscow 1988, p 125.

JOSEF HOFMANN

Rakhmaninov was made out of steel and gold: steel in his hands – gold in his heart. I cannot think of him without tears. Not only did I admire him as a great artist but I loved him as a man.

Pamiati S V Rakhmaninova / Memories of S V Rakhmaninov, ed M V Dobuzhinsky, New York 1946, p 36.

THEODOR W ADORNO

There are passages in his works for young people and for student concerts which are grandiose and over-written. Small hands make a show of being strong; children imitate adults – wherever possible virtuosos who are swotting up on Liszt. It all sounds extremely heavy and in any case very loud. But is it sadly easy; a child player well knows that stupendous passages cannot go wrong and is sure in advance of an effortless triumph. Rakhmaninov's C sharp minor Prelude provides infantile adults with the same childish triumph. It owes its popularity to listeners who identify with the player and know they could play it just as well. In marvelling at the power which masters the four-note chords in fourfold fortissimo, they are marvelling at themselves. In their imagination they grow massive hands. Psychoanalysts discovered the Nero complex; the Prelude already exemplified it.

Musikalische Warenanalysen / Musical Textual Analysis, in *Gesammelte Schriften / Collected Writings*, ed Rolf Tiedemann, Frankfurt-am-Main 1978, p 285.

List of Works

Works which were only planned, are not available or not edited are not mentioned in this list, nor are piano reductions of works by other composers or arrangements (harmonisations) of Russian folk songs. Second versions or arrangements of his own works are only mentioned as exceptions. The dates refer to the year of composition. Further information can be found in the Threlfall/Norris publication *A Catalogue of the Compositions* (see Bibliography).

I Works op 1 to op 45

op 1 Concerto no 1 for piano and orchestra, F-sharp minor, 1890/91 (second ed 1917).

op 2 Two Pieces for cello and piano, 1892. 1 Prelude, F major; 2 Oriental Dance, A minor.

op 3 Five *Morceaux de Fantaisie* for piano, 1892. 1 Elegy, E-flat minor; 2 Prelude, C-sharp minor; 3 Melody, E major (2nd edition 1940); 4 Serenade, B-flat minor (2nd edition 1940), 4 Polichinella, F-sharp minor; 5 Serenade, B-flat minor (2nd edition 1940).

op 4 Six Songs with piano accompaniment, 1890–93. 1 *O net, molyu, nye uchodi / O no, I beg you, do not go* (D S Merezkovsky); 2 *Utro / Morning* (M N Janov); 3 *V molchani nochi tainoy/ In the silence of mysterious night* (A A Fet); 4 *Nye poy, krasavitsa / Do not sing, lovely one* (A S Pushkin); 5 *Uzh ty, niva moja / O you, my meadow* (A K Tolstoy); 6 *Davno ly, moy drug / How long ago, my friend* (A A Golyenishchev-Kutuzov).

op 5 Fantaisie-Tableaux (Suite 1) for two pianos, 1893. 1 Barcarolle, G minor; 2 *I noch, i lyubov/ Night, and love,* G major; 3 *Slyetsy / Tears,* G minor; 4 S*vyetly pratzdnik / Easter Holiday,* G minor.

op 6 Two Pieces for violin and piano, 1893. 1 Romance, D minor; 2 Hungarian Dance, D minor.

op 7 Fantasy for orchestra *Uyos / The Cliff* (after M J Lermontov), B minor, 1893.

op 8 Six songs with piano accompaniment, transl A N Pleshchev, 1893. 1 *Rechnaya lileya / The Waterlily* (H Heine); 2 *Ditya! Kak tsvetok ty prekrasna / Child: you are as lovely as a flower* (H Heine); 3 *Duma / Thought* (T G Shevchenko); 4 *Polyubila ya na pyechel svoyu / I found delight in my grief* (T G Shevchenko); 5 *Son / Dream* (H Heine); 6 *Molitva / Prayer* (J W v Goethe).

op 9 Trio Élégiaque for piano, violin and cello, D minor, 1893.

op 10 Seven *Morceaux de Salon* for piano, 1893/94. 1 Nocturne, A minor; 2 Waltz, A major; 3 Barcarolle, G minor; 4 Melody, E minor; 5 Humoresque, G major; 6 Romance, E major; 7 Mazurka, D-flat major.

op 11 Six pieces for piano (4 hands), 1894. 1 Barcarolle, G minor; 2 Scherzo, D major; 3 Russian Song, B minor; 4 Waltz, A major; 5 Romance, C minor; 6 *Slava / Glory*, C major.

op 12 Capriccio on gypsy themes for orchestra, B minor, 1894.

op 13 Symphony no 1, D minor, for orchestra, 1895.

op 14 Twelve songs with piano accompaniment, 1896. 1 *Ya zhdu tyebya / I wait for thee* (M A Davidova; 2 *Ostrovok / The Isle* (P B Shelley; transl K D Balmont); 3 *Davno v lyubvi otrady malo / For long has love brought little comfort* (A A Fet); 4 *Ya byl u ney / I was with her* (A V Koltsov); 5 *Eti lyetnye nochy / These summer nights* (D M Rathaus); 6 *Tyebya tak liubiat vse / Everyone loves you so* (A K Tolstoy); 7 *Nye ver mnye, drug / O friend, do not believe me* (A K Tolstoy); 8 *O, nye grusti / Oh, be not sad* (A N Apukhtin); 9 *Ona, kak poldyen, khorosha / She is lovely as the noon* (N M Minsky); 10 *V moy dushe / In my soul* (N M Minsky); 11 *Vyesyennie vodi / Waters of spring* (F I Tyuchev); 12 *Pora! / It is time!* (S J Nadson).

op 15 Six Choruses for women's or children's choirs with piano accompaniment, 1894/6. 1 *Slavsya / Be praised* (N A Nekrasov); 2 *Nochka / Night* (V N Lodyzhensky); 3 *Sosna / The Pine tree* (M J Lermontov); 4 *Zadremali volny / The waves fell asleep* (Romanov); 5 *Nevyolya / Slavery* (N G Tsyganov); 6 *Angel* (M J Lermontov).

op 16 Six *Moments Musicaux* for piano, 1896. 1 B-flat minor; 2 E-flat minor (2nd edition 1940); 3 B minor; 4 E minor; 5 D-sharp major; 6 C major.

op 17 Suite 2 for two pianos, 1900/1. 1 Introduction C major; 2 Waltz G major; 3 Romance A-flat major; 4 Tarantella C minor.

op 18 Concerto no 2 for piano and orchestra, C minor, 1900/1.

op 19 Sonata for cello and piano, G minor, 1901.

op 20 *Vesna / Spring*. Cantata for baritone, chorus and orchestra, poem *Zelyoniy shum / Verdant rustling* (N A Nekrasov), E major, 1902.

op 21 12 Songs with piano accompaniment, 1900/2. 1 *Sudba / Fate* (A N Apukhtin); 2 *Nad svyezhey mogiloy / On a fresh grave* (S J Nadson); 3 *Sumerki / Twilight* (M Guyot, transl M Chorzhevsky); 4 *Oni otvyechali / They replied* (V Hugo, transl L A Mey); 5 *Siren / Lilac* (E A Beketova); 6 *Otryvok iz A Miusse / Fragment from de Musset* (transl Apukhtin); 7 *Zdyes khorosho / How fair is this place* (G A Galina); 8 *Na smert shizhika / On the Death of a linnet* (V A Zhukovsky); 9 *Melodya / Melody* (S J Nadson); 10 *Pryed ikonoy / Before the ikon* (A A Golenishchev-Kutuzov; 11 *Ya nye prorok / I am no prophet* (A V Kruglov); 12 *Kak mnye bolno / How it pains me* (G A Galina).

op 22 Variations on a theme by Chopin for piano, C minor, 1902/3.

op 23 10 Preludes for piano, 1903. 1 F-sharp minor; 2 B-flat major; 3 D minor; 4 D major; 5 G minor; 6 E-flat major; 7 C minor; 8 A-flat major; 9 E-flat minor; 10 G-flat major.

op 24 *Skupoy rytsar / The Miserly Knight*, one-act opera in three scenes after the *Little Tragedy* by A S Pushkin, 1903/4.

op 25 *Francesca da Rimini,* one-act opera in two scenes with prologue and epilogue. Libretto by M I Tchaikovsky after Dante Alighieri's *Divina Commedia*, Canto V of *Inferno*, 1904/5.

op 26 15 Songs with piano accompaniment, 1906. 1 *Yest mnogo zvukov / There are many sounds* (A K Tolstoy); 2 *Vsyo otnial u menya / He took all from me* (F I Tyuchev); 3 *My otdokhnym / Let us rest* (A P Chekhov); 4 *Dva proshchanya / Two farewells* (A V Koltsov); 5 *Pokinem, milaya / Let us go, beloved* (A A Golenishchev-Kutuzov); 6 *Christos voskres / Christ is risen* (D S Merezhkovsky); 7 *K dyetyam / For the children* (A S Khomiakov); 8 *Poshchadi ya molyu! / I beg for mercy!* D S Merezhkovsky); 9 *Ya opiat odinok / I am once more alone* (T G Shevchenko, transl I A Bunin); 10 *U moyevo okna / At my window* (G A Galina); 11 *Fontan / The fountain* (F I Tyuchev);

12 *Noch pechalna / Sorrowful night* (I A Bunin); 13 *Vchera my vstretilis / Yesterday we met* (Y P Polonsky); 14 *Koltso / The ring* (A V Koltsov); 15 *Prokhodit vsyo / Everything fades away* (D M Rathaus).

op 27 Symphony no 2, E minor, 1906/7.

op 28 Piano Sonata no 1, D minor, 1907.

op 29 *Ostrov myortvykh / The Isle of the Dead*, symphonic poem for orchestra in A minor after the eponymous painting by Arnold Böcklin, 1909.

op 30 Concerto no 3 for piano and orchestra, D minor, 1909.

op 31 *Liturgiy sviatovo Ioanna Zlatousta / Liturgy of St John Chrysostom* for chorus a cappella, 1910.

op 32 13 Preludes for piano, 1910. 1 C major; 2 B-flat minor; 3 E major; 4 E minor; 5 G major; 6 F minor; 7 F major; 8 A minor; 9 A major; 10 B minor; 11 B major; 12 G-sharp minor; 13 D-flat major.

op 33 Six *Études-Tableaux* for piano, 1911. 1 F minor; 2 C major; 3 E-flat minor; 4 E-flat major; 5 G minor; 6 C-sharp minor.

(Three further *Études* from 1911 were not included in op 33: A minor (orig op 33, no 4) appears in revised form as op 39, no 6. C minor and D minor (orig op 33, nos 3 & 5) published posthumously.

op 34 14 Songs with piano accompaniment, 1912. 1 *Muza / The muse* (A S Pushkin); 2 *V dushe u kashdovo iz nas / In the soul of each of us* (A A Korinfsky); 3 *Burya / The storm* (A S Pushkin); 4 *Veter perelyotny / Flying wind* (K D Balmont); 5 *Arion* (A S Pushkin); 6 *Voskresenye Lazaria / The raising of Lazarus* (A S Khomiakov); 7 *Ne mozhet byt / It cannot be* (A N Maikov); 8 *Muzyka / Music* (Y P Polonsky); 9 *Ty znal yevo / You knew him* (F I Tiuchev); 10 *Sey denya pomnyu / I remember that day* (F I Tyuchev); 11 *Obrochnik / The peasant* (A A Fet); 12 *Kakoe schastye / What happiness* (A A Fet); 13 *Dissonans / Dischord* (Y P Polonsky); 14 *Vokaliz / Vocalise.*

op 35 *Kolokola / The Bells*, poem for soloists, chorus and orchestra after Edgar Allen Poe, transl K D Balmont, 1913.

op 36 Piano Sonata 2 B-flat minor, 1913 (2nd edition 1931).

op 37 *Vsenoshchnoye vdenye / Vespers (All-night Vigil)*. Russian Orthodox Church vigil with evening and morning prayers. Old church tunes and settings of old church texts arr chorus a cappella, 1915.

op 38 Six Songs with piano accompaniment, 1916. 1 *Nochyu v sadu u menya* / *At night in my garden* (after A Isaakian, transl A A Blok); 2 *K ney* / *To her* (A Bely); 3 *Margaritki* / *Marguerites* (I Severianin); 4 *Krysolov* / *The Rat catcher* (V Y Briusov); 5 *Son* / *A dream* (F K Sollohub); 6 *A-u!* (K D Balmont).

op 39 Nine *Études-Tableaux* for piano, 1916/17. 1 C minor; 2 A minor; 3 F-sharp minor; 4 B-flat minor; 5 E-flat minor; 6 A minor (orig version 1911 intended for op 33); 7 C minor; 8 D minor; 9 D major.

op 40 Fourth Piano Concerto, G minor, 1926 (2nd edition, 1941).

op 41 Three Russian Songs for chorus and orchestra, 1926. 1 *Cherez ryechku, yrechku bystru* / *Over the river, the swift river*; 2 *Akh ty, Vanka, razudala golova* / *Ah Vanka, you bold leader*; 3 *Byelilitsy, rumianitsy vy moy* / *Whiten my rosy cheeks.*

op 42 Variations on a theme by Corelli for piano, D minor, 1931.

op 43 Rhapsody on a theme by Paganini for piano and orchestra, A minor, 1934.

op 44 Symphony no 3, A minor, 1935/6.

op 45 Symphonic Dances for orchestra, 1940.

II Works without opus number, published by the composer

Songs without words for piano D minor, 1887.

Aleko, one-act opera. Libretto by V I Nemirovich-Danchenko after *Tsygany* / *The Gypsies* (A S Pushkin), 1892.

Panteley-tsyelitel / *Panteley the healer* (A K Tolstoy) for chorus a cappella, 1899/1901.

Noch / *Night* (D M Rathaus). Song with piano accompaniment, 1900.

Polka italienne for piano (4 hands), 1906.

Pismo K S Stanislavskomu ot S V Rakhmaninova / *Letter to K S Stanislavsky from S V Rakhmaninov.* Song with piano accompaniment, 1908.

Polka V R for piano, 1911. 'The composer's father, V A Rakhmaninov, who was inclined to fantasise, let his son believe that the polka he often played to the family was his own composition. In fact it was published in the musical appendix to the journal *Nuvellist* 10/1875 pp 475–79 as op 303 of the composer F Behr, entitled *La Rieuse. Polka Badine / The laughing woman. A humorous polka.*' (Z Apetyan, *Vospominania / Recollections*, vol 2, Moscow 1988, p 480.)

Iz evangelia ot Ioanna / From St John's Gospel. Song with piano accompaniment, 1915.

Fragments for piano A-flat major, 1917.

Vostochniy eskits / Oriental sketch for piano B-flat major, 1917.

III Works Published Posthumously

PIANO MUSIC
Four pieces, 1887 (or later). 1 Romance F-sharp minor; 2 Prelude E-flat minor; 3 Melody E major; 4 Gavotte D major.

Three Nocturnes, 1887/8. 1 F-sharp minor; 2 F major; 3 C minor.

Canon D minor, ?1890/1

Prelude F major (op 2 no 1 in piano version) 1891.

Cadenza to Liszt's 2nd Hungarian Rhapsody, 1919.

Combined composition with A Arensky, A Glazunov and S Taneyev: Four Improvisations, 1896. [All four composers contributed to each number.]

Romance for piano (4 hands) G major, 1894?

Two Pieces for piano (6 hands), 1890/1. 1 Waltz, A major; 2 Romance, A major.

Russkaya rapsoda / Russian Rhapsody for two pianos, 1891.

CHAMBER MUSIC
Romance for violin and piano A minor, 1888.

Song for cello and piano, F minor, 1890.

Melody for cello or violin and piano D major, 1890.

Two movements of unfinished *1st String Quartet*: *Andante* (Romance), G minor; *Scherzo*, D major, 1889.

Two movements of unfinished 2nd String Quartet: 1 G minor; 2 C minor, 1896.

Trio Élégiaque [1] for piano, violin and cello, G minor, 1892.

SINGLE SONGS WITH PIANO ACCOMPANIMENT
U vrat obiteli sviatoy / At the door of the holy dwelling (M J Lermontov), 1890.

Ya tebe nichevo ne skazhu / I shall tell you nothing (A A Fet) ,1890.

Opiat vstrepenulos ty, serdtse / Once more you leapt, my heart (N P Grekov), 1890.

C'était en avril / It was in April (Edouard Pailleron, transl V Tusnovaya: *Aprel! Vesnji prazdnichni den*), 1891.

Smerkalos / Twilight has fallen (A K Tolstoy), 1891.

Ty pomnish ly vecher / Do you remember the evening (A K Tolstoy), 1891.

Pesnya razocharovannovo / Song of the disillusioned man (D M Rathaus), 1893.

Uvial cvetok / The flower is faded (D M Rathaus), 1893.

Ikalos ly tebe / Did you have hiccups? [Joking song] (P A Viazemsky), 1899.

Molitva / The prayer (K Romanov), 1916.

Vsyo khochet pet / Everything wants to sing (F Sollohub), 1916.

A CAPPELLA CHORUSES
Deus meus / My God, six-part motet, 1890.

V molitvakh neusypaiushchuyu bogorodicu / Beseechng the Virgin unceasingly in prayer, Sacred concerto (motet), 1893.

Chor dukhov / Chorus of spirits, after *Don Juan* (A K Tolstoy), 1894?

ORCHESTRAL
Scherzo in D minor, 1887.

Youthful Symphony in D minor (first movement), 1891.

Knyaz Rostislav / Prince Rostislav. Symphonic poem after ballad (A K Tolstoy), 1891.

Arbenin's Monologue from the play *Maskarad / Masquerade* by M J Lermontov: *Noch, provedennaya bez sna / Night, passed without sleep* set for bass and piano, 1890/1.

Two monologues from the play *Boris Godunov* by A S Pushkin: Boris's monologue *Ty, otche patriarch / Oh thou, father patriarch* (3 versions) for bass and piano; Pimen's monologue *Eshche odno posledney skazany / One last story* (2 versions) for tenor and piano, 1890/1.

IV Piano Transcriptions

Bach, J S: Prelude, gavotte and gigue from E major Partita for solo violin, 1933.

Bizet, G: Minuet from *L'Arlesienne* Suite 2 for A Daudet's play, 1900 (revised early 1920s).

Tchaikovsky, P: Lullaby, Romance op 16 1 (A N Maikov), 1941.

Kreisler, F: *Liebesleid*, 1921; *Liebesfreud*, 1925.

Mendelssohn, F: *Scherzo* from the music for Shakespeare's *Midsummer Night's Dream*, 1933.

Mussorgsky, M: *Hopak* from the opera *The Fair at Sorochinsk*, 1923.

Rimsky-Korsakov, N: *The flight of the bumblebee* from the opera *The legend of Tsar Saltan*, 1929.

Schubert, F: *Wohin? / Whither?* From *Die schöne Müllerin*, 1925.

V Recordings

Full information on Rakhmaninov's recordings can be found in Barrie Martyn's book (see Bibliography). The following edition gives an impression of his interpretation:
Sergei Rakhmaninov – The complete recordings (10 CDs) [RCA Victor Gold Seal 09026 61265 2].

Selected Discography

SYMPHONIES AND ORCHESTRAL WORKS

Symphonies Nos. 1 – 3. Berlin Philharmonic Orchestra/ Lorin Maazel (cond). Deutsche Grammophon DG 445 590- 2 (2 CD)

Symphonie No. 2; The Rock Op 7. Russian National Orchestra/ Mikhail Pletnev (cond). Deutsche Grammophon DG 439 888 2

Symphonic Dances, Op 45; The Isle of the Dead, Op 29. Royal Philharmonic Orchestra/ Enrique Bátiz (cond). Naxos 8. 530 583

PIANO CONCERTOS

Piano Concertos Nos. 1 – 4. Vladimir Ashkenazy (pf)/ London Symphony Orchestra/ André Previn (cond). Decca 444839 (2 CD)

Piano Concertos Nos. 1 & 2. Krystian Zimmerman (pf)/ Boston Symphony Orchestra/ Seiji Ozawa (cond) . Deutsche Grammophon DG 459 643-2

Piano Concerto No 3. Vladimir Horowitz (pf)/ New York Philharmonic Orchestra/ Sir John Barbirolli (cond). *(Historic live recording)* APR mono 5519

PIANO MUSIC

The Complete Solo Piano Music. Howard Shelley (pf). Hyperion CDS44041/8 (8CD)

Etudes Tableaux, Op 33, Preludes Op. 23 (*excerpts*). Nikolai Demidenko (pf). Hyperion CDA 66713

Piano Transcriptions and Arrangements. Idil Biret (pf). Naxos 8.550978

CHAMBER MUSIC

Piano Trios Nos. 1 & 2. Beaux Arts Trio. Philips 420175

Complete Works for Cello and Piano (Sonata Op. 14 etc.). Michael Grebanier (vc)/ Janet Guggenheim (pf). Naxos 8.550987

SONGS

Complete Songs Vol. 3. Joan Rodgers (sop)/ Maria Popescu (mez)/ Alexandre Naoumenko (ten)/ Sergei Leiferkus (bar)/ Howard Shelly (pf). Chandos Chan 9477

SACRED MUSIC

Verspers, op. 37. Swedish Radio Choir/ Tonu Kaljuste (cond). Virgin Classics 5618452

Liturgy of St. John Chrysostom. Chorus of the Bulgarian Radio/ Mihkil Milkov (cond). EMI 7243 5 686642 3 (2 CD)

OPERA

Aleko Pavel Kuchunov (ten)/ Blagovesta Karnoblatova (sop)/ Dimiter Petkov (bass)/ Plovdiv Philharmonic Orchestra & Choir/ Rousian Raychev (cond). Capriccio Records 10782

RAKHMANINOV PLAYS RAKHMANINOV

Piano Concertos Nos. 1–4; Rhapsody on a theme of Paganini. Sergei Rakhmaninov (pf)/ The Philadelphia Orchestra/ Eugene Ormandy (cond) & Leopold Stokowski (cond). *(Recorded 1929–1941)* RCA Victor/ Red Seal 09026 61658 2 (2 CD)

Symphony No. 3; The Isle of the Dead, Op 29; Vocalise The Philadelphia Orchestra/ Sergei Rakhmaninov (cond). *(Historic recording)* RCA Victor/ Red Seal 09026 625322

The Complete Recordings. (includes also works by other composers performed by Rakhmaninov). *(Recorded 1919–1942)* RCA Victor/ Golden Seal RCA 09026 611256 2 (10 CD)

About the Author

Andreas Wehrmeyer was born in 1959 and studied musicology, history and German language and literature in Münster and Berlin. In 1990 his thesis on *Russian Musical Thought about 1920* (Frankfurt-am-Main etc 1991) gained him an appointment as lector and writer for radio at the Berlin Technical University and as an associate lecturer at musical colleges and at the University. His main fields are 18th- and 19th-century music, music theory and Russian music. His publications are mostly on the subject of Russian and 20th-century music. In 1994/5 he spent a year in Moscow on a grant from the Alexander von Humboldt Institute.

Picture Sources

The author and publishers wish to express their thanks to the following sources of illustrative material and/or permission to reproduce it. They will make proper acknowledgements in futue editions in the event that any omissions have occurred.

Bridgeman Art Library: pp. 34, 53, 95; Cornelius Schnauber, Los Angeles: pp. 111; Glinka Museum, Moscow: pp. 70, 72; Heritage Image Pictures: pp. 45, 50, 86; Lebrecht Music Collection: pp. 7, 9, 14, 19, 26, 29, 33, 36, 38, 40, 43, 59, 61, 62, 66, 68, 78, 83, 100, 101, 102, 103, 112; Novosti: pp. 1, 2, 6, 56, 74, 96, 99; Stefan Weidle, Bonn (Eric Schaal): pp. 92, 114; Süddeutscher Verlag, Munich: pp. 23.

Index

harmony, 26

Haydn, Franz Joseph, 94

Heifetz, Jascha, 84

Hertenstein, 101

Hindemith, Paul, ix

Hofmann, Josef, viii, 88, 91, 98; biography, 58

Holland, 56

Horovitz, Vladimir, viii, 59–60, 65, 73, 109; biography, 59

hypnosis, 36

Igumnov, Konstantin, 54

Italian Riviera, 100

Italy, 49

Ivanovka, 14–15, 58, 85, 101

jazz, 103

Karatygin, Viacheslav, ix, 65

Kashkin, Nikolay, 37, 45

Kastalsky, Alexander, 76

Kensico Cemetery, 113

Kersin, M and Mme, 57

Kharkov, 110

Kiev, 8, 18, 71, 110

Koons, Walter, 113

Korovin, Konstantin, 31

Koshets, Nina, 82, 83, 84–5

Koussevitsky, Sergey, 48, 64, 80, 88–9

Kreisler, Fritz, 59, 88, 106; biography, 88

Kreyn, Grigory, 64

Kruglikov, Semyon, 18

Lake Lucerne, 101, 102

Leipzig, 51

Leningrad, 65, 110

Lermontov, Mikhail Yurevich, 35

Leschetizky, Theodor, 87

Liszt, Franz, 4, 10, 13, 25, 65, 75, 91, 94, 96; influence on Rakhmaninov, 24, 51, 53, 94–5; metamorphosis technique, 51; *La Campanella*, 93; *Totentanz*, 95, 107, 108; *Waldesrauschen*, 93

London, 35, 56, 68

Long Island, 110, 111

Maeterlinck, Maurice, 49

Mahler, Gustav, 63, 72

Mamontov, Sava, 31–2, 44

Mamontov Private Opera, 31–2, 33, 34, 44, 48

Mascagni, Pietro, 17

Masel, Lev, 133–4

Medtner, Emil, 67–8

Medtner, Nikolay, viii, xiv, 47, 67–8, 91, 94, 105; biography, 68; Rakhmaninov pays fee, 105; aversion to 'moderns', 106; First Piano Sonata op 5, 67; *The Muse and the Fashion*, 68

melody, x, 37, 41, 113

Mendelssohn, Felix, 94

Miaskovsky, Nikolay, 72

'mighty handful', 22

modernism, vii–ix, 64–5, 66, 80, 105

Moiseiwitsch, Benno, 35

Morosov, Nikita, 54, 55, 110

Moscow, 14, 16, 21, 22, 33, 36, 55, 57, 71, 85, 104, 110; Historical Concerts, 11; Tchaikovsky Competition, 59; musical life,

Concerts, 10, 11

Rubinstein, Arthur, 135

Rubinstein, Nikolay, 13, 19, 25

Russia, x, 2, 48; popularity of Italian opera, 17; rival musical capitals, 22; railways, 31; 1905 Revolution, 49; 1917 Revolutions, xi, 65, 76, 79, 85, 89; cut off by war, 79, 110–11; Civil War, 89, 110

Russian culture, 31, 42, 99, 100, 104

Russian music, 24, 55, 57, 62–3, 104; establishment, 64; *see also* church music; folk music

Russian Music Publishing House, 64, 66, 82

Russian Music Society, 57, 64

Russian News, 81

Russian Orthodox Church, 75; liturgy, 8, 62, 76; *see also* church music

Russian School, 3

Sabaneyev, Leonid, 65, 100

Safonov, Vassily, 11, 15, 48

St Petersburg, 3, 55, 65, 85; Ziloti concert series, 13; premiere of First Symphony, 22

St Petersburg Conservatory, 4, 5–6, 8, 10, 25;

Saint-Saëns, Camille, 32

Saklon, Vera, 15

Satin family, 14–15, 36, 38–9, 100

Satina, Sophia, 13, 20, 39

Satina, Varvara Arkadievna, 13

Scarlatti, Domenico, 94

Schnabel, Artur, viii

Schoenberg, Arnold, ix, 105

Schonberg, Harold, 97

Schor, David, 18

Schubert, Franz, 94; *Plainte d'une jeune fille*, 5

Schuch, Ernst Edler von, 50

Schumann, Robert, 94; Piano Concerto, 95

Scriabin, Alexander, ix, xiv, 11, 13, 26, 55, 65–7, 94, 113; focus for 'modernism', 64; death, 79; memorial concerts, 80–1; on Rakhmaninov, 81; Fifth Piano Sonata, 94; Mysterium, 80; Piano Concerto in F-sharp minor op 20, 66; *Poem of Fire*, 67; *Prometheus*, 67

Second World War, 112

Semyonovo, 2

Senar, 101–2, 110

Serov, Valentin, 31

Severianin, Igor, 84

Shaginian, Marietta, 68, 69–70, 82; Communism, 70

Shakespeare, William, 91

Shostakovich, Dmitri Dmitriyevich, ix

Sibelius, Jean Julius Christian, 13

Skalon, General, 15

Skalon, Natalya, 29

Smolensky, Stephan, 76

Society of Lovers of Russian Music, 57

sonata, 41

Soviet Union, 110–11

Stalin, 70

Stanislavsky, Konstantin, 33

Staraya Russa region, 1

Steinway, 59

Stockholm, 87

Strauss, Richard, ix, 50; *Salome*, 50
Stravinsky, Igor, ix, 13, 105; meets Rakhmaninov, 111–12; *Firebird*, 112; *Petrushka*, 112; *The Rite of Spring*, 82, 112
Sweden, 85
Switzerland, 49, 70, 101
symbolists, 82–3

Tair Publishers, 100
Tambov region, 1, 14
Taneyev, Sergey Ivanovich, 11, 12, 20, 23, 57, 65, 94, 95, 113; influence on Rakhmaninov, 25; on Rakhmaninov's Second Piano Concerto, 37; dedicatee of Rakhmaninov's Second Symphony, 51–2; death, 81; monograph on, 100; *John of Damascus*, 42
tastiera per luce, 67
Tausig, Karl, 94
Tchaikovsky, Pyotr Ilyich, viii, ix, 4, 11, 12, 13, 113; influence on Rakhmaninov, 16, 17, 19, 23, 27; death, 18–19; compositional principles, 25; Fifth Symphony, 51; *Liturgy* op 41, 76; *Moscow*, 42; *Eugene Onegin*, 46; Piano Trio op 50, 19; *Queen of Spades*, 46; Sixth Symphony *Pathétique*, 18, 72; *Vespers*, 76

Tolstoy, Leo, 34–5
Tua, Teresina, 21

USA, *see* America

Victory Day, 62
Vienna, 3
Viennese School, 105
Villoing, Alexandre, 10
Volga, River, 2, 80
Vrubel, Mikhail, 31

Wagner, Richard, 25, 72
Warsaw, 56
Weber, Carl Maria von, 94
Webern, Anton, ix, 105
Weimar, 4
Wolkonsky, Count Peter, 99

Yalta, 34

Ziloti, Alexander, xiv, 4, 8, 11, 15, 24, 35, 91, 95; biography, 13; conducts Rakhmaninov's Second Piano Concerto, 37
Zimbalist, Efrem, 88
Zverev, Nikolay Sergeyevich, xiii, 8–13, 65; break with Rakhmaninov, 12–13; reconciliation with Rakhmaninov, 16

LIFE & TIMES FROM HAUS

Churchill
by Sebastian Haffner
'One of the most brilliant things of
any length ever written about
Churchill.' *TLS*
1-904341-07-1 (pb) £8.99
1-904341-06-3 (hb) £12.99

Dietrich
by Malene Skaerved
'It is probably the best book ever on
Marlene.' C. Downes
1-904341-13-6 (pb) £8.99
1-904341-12-8 (hb) £12.99

Beethoven
by Martin Geck
'...this little gem is a truly handy reference.' *Musical Opinion*
1-904341-00-4 (pb) £8.99
1-904341-03-9 (hb) £12.99

Prokofiev
by Thomas Schipperges
'beautifully made, ... well-produced
photo-graphs, ... with useful historical nuggets.' *The Guardian*
1-904341-32-2 (pb) £8.99
1-904341-34-9 (hb) £12.99

Curie
by Sarah Dry
'...this book could hardly be bettered' *New Scientist*
selected as **Outstanding Academic Title** by *Choice*
1-904341-29-2 (pb) £8.99

Einstein
by Peter D Smith
'Concise, complete, well-produced and lively throughout, ... a bargain at the price.' *New Scientist*
1-904341-15-2 (pb) £8.99
1-904341-14-4 (hb) £12.99

Casement
by Angus Mitchell
'hot topic' *The Irish Times*
1-904341-41-1 (pb) £8.99

Britten
by David Matthews
'I have read them all - but none with as much enjoyment as this.' *Literary Review*
1-904341-21-7 (pb) £8.99
1-904341-39-X (hb) £12.99

De Gaulle
by Julian Jackson
'this concise and distinguished
book' Andrew Roberts *Sunday
Telegraph*
1-904341-44-6 (pb) £8.99

Orwell
by Scott Lucas
'short but controversial assessment
... is sure to raise a few eyebrows'
Sunday Tasmanian
1-904341-33-0 (pb) £8.99

Bach
by Martin Geck
'The production values of the book
are exquisite, too.'
The Guardian
1-904341-16-0 (pb) £8.99
1-904341-35-7 (hb) £12.99

Kafka
by Klaus Wagenbach
'One of the most useful books about
Kafka ever published' *Frankfurter
Allgemeine Zeitung*
1-904341-02 -0 (PB) £8.99
1-904341-01-2 (hb) £12.99

Dostoevsky
by Richard Freeborn
'... wonderful ... a learned guide' *The Sunday Times*
1-904341-27-6 (pb) £8.99

Brahms
by Hans Neunzig
'readable, comprehensive and attractively priced'
The Irish Times
1-904341-17-9 (pb) £8.99

Verdi
by Barbara Meier
'These handy volumes fill a gap in the market ... admirably.' *Classic fM*
1-904341-21-7 (pb) £8.99
1-904341-39-X (hb) L12.99

Armstrong
by David Bradbury
'generously illustrated ... a fine and well-researched introduction' George Melly *Daily Mail*
1-904341-46-2 (pb) £8.99
1-904341-47-0 (hb) £12.99